LIMITS OF REPRESENTATION

Edited by Franco Farinelli, Gunnar Olsson and Dagmar Reichert

1994

Studies of Action and Organization (SAO),
Vol. 5 (A Publication of the
European Centre of Arts and Management)

Distributed in the U.S.A. by
The Institute of Mind and Behavior
P.O. Box 522, Village Station
New York City, NY 10014

© 1994, Accedo Verlagsgesellschaft mbH
Gnesener Str. 1, D-81929 Munich, FRG.

ISBN 3-89265-017-9
Cover: Hannes Hein (Collage Komplott)
Printed by U. Novotny, Starnberg, FRG.

Contents

Preface	5
Acknowledgements	6

Squaring the circle, or the nature of political identity *Franco Farinelli*	11
Chiasm of thought-and-action *Gunnar Olsson*	29
Red river valley: Geo-graphical studies in the landscape of language Ole Michael Jensen	57
Rites of tresspassing *Dagmar Reichert and Ole Michael Jensen*	67
The woman as utopia *Dagmar Reichert*	81
The form of relatedness *Mario Neve*	101
Finite specificity *Ulf Strohmayer and Matthew Hannah*	115
Spaces of misrepresentation *Peter Gould*	122
The moral power of representation: Rationality, trust and urban conflict Ola Söderström	155
Do you think Columbus could have been a woman? *Verena Meier*	175
(Re)constructively re-presenting the present, image-ining the contemporary world, resonating with the condition(ing)s of hypermodernity *Allan Pred*	181
Global and local geo-graphies *Giuseppe Dematteis*	199

Epilogue	217

List of contributors	221

PREFACE

When and where did it start? Whence and whither will it go? Impossible to tell, for only material things, not human relations, can be caught in the Kantian coordinate net of time and space. Our eyes are not ours alone.

And yet. Even in the absence of beginnings and ends, there are stages on life's way. The present book is no exception, for it is an objective correlate of recurring conversations here and there, now and then. More precisely, the thirteen chapters which follow are all connected with the last week of June, 1991. It was then that the themes of limits and representations once more brought our group together, this time in the mysterious Villa Clarke on the outskirts of Bagni di Lucca. The villa, and the hospitality which came with it, was put at our disposal by the University of Bologna. Without the determined efforts of Franco Farinelli, the Italian comforts would not have been ours. Without the editorial persistence of Dagmar Reichert, this art-filled volume would not now be yours.

The eleven who gathered in Bagni di Lucca are not obedient representatives but independent individuals, not a soccer team but long-distance runners. What ties us together is a double bond of friendship and a common background in the theory of geography and the practice of mapping. It is this fusion of the personal and the professional that makes our reunions so worthwhile, for whereas pure intuition is intra-subjective, spatial intuition is inter-subjective.

But: How does spatial intuition express itself in the current world of hypermodernity? Why would just we succeed in liberating ourselves from the reflective images of Plato's cave, when noone else ever has? Which are the differences between a presentation, a representation, and a representation of a representation? Is it at all possible to think the limit of a limit and to communicate the same?

If these are the questions, there may be no answers. Perhaps our whole endeavor was foreshadowed by Raymond Roussel, who entitled one of his books *Comment j'ai écrit certains de mes livres*. The point is not made, the point makes itself. What cannot be said can sometimes be shown. What must not be asked may sometimes be done.

Gunnar Olsson

ACKNOWLEDGEMENTS

The cover picture by Florent *La terre et ses ramifications internes* and the pictures on p.9 Kouw *Paysage autour d'une sphere*, p.55 Robert Gie *Systeme cosmique de circulation d'efluves*, p.99 Josef Heuer *Buste compose en carte de suisse*, p.153 Johann *Deux paysages alpins*, p.215 Sylvain *"L'art reigne eh dans l'plat fond"* were reprinted by permission of the Collection de l'art brut, Lausanne. We would like to thank Ms. Geneviève Roulin for her kind help with the selection of the pictures.

The text of "Chiasm of thought-and-action" first appeared in Society and Space, Vol. 11/3 , and was reprinted by permission of Pion Ltd., London. Claude Mellan's self-referential version of Veronica's kerchief was reproduced by permission of Göteborgs Konstmuseum, Göteborg.

The text "Red river valley" first appeared in Society and Space, Vol. 11/3, and was reprinted by permission of Pion Ltd, London. The maps were drawn by Henning Holmsted, and the block diagrams of Axel Schou *The Construction and Drawing of Block Diagrams* (1962) were reprinted by permission of Thomas Nelson and Sons Ltd., Edinburgh.

The woodcut *Schadenzaubertaten der Hexen* (1511) in the chapter "Rites of tresspassing" was reprinted by permission of the Archiv für Kunst und Geschichte, Berlin. The picture of the *Chimera*, was reprinted by permission of the Musèe G. Moreau, Paris.

The text "Woman as Utopia" first appeared in Gender, Place and Culture, Vol. 1/1994, and was reprinted by permission of Carfax Publishing Company, Abingdon.

The map of the planning project (Figure 1) in the chapter "Moral power of representation: Rationality, trust and urban conflict" was reprinted from L'Habitation 3/4, 1991.

The photograph *Children in Bocas de Satinga, Colombia* in the chapter

"Do you think Columbus could have been a woman" was taken by H. Buschor and was printed by his permission.

Last but not least we would like to thank the Swiss Academy of Sciences, the Swiss Federal Institute of Technology, the Nordplan Institute in Stockholm, and the Danish Building Research Institute for supporting the editing of this book.

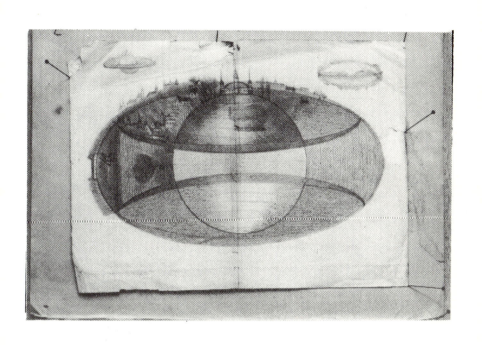

Kouw: *Paysage autour d'une sphere*

SQUARING THE CIRCLE, OR THE NATURE OF POLITICAL IDENTITY

by Franco Farinelli

> *The doctrine of Right and Wrong is perpetually disputed, both by the Pen and the Sword: Whereas the doctrine of Lines, and Figures, is not so; because men care not, in that subject what be truth, as a thing that crosses no man ambition, profit, or lust. For I doubt not, but if it had been a thing contrary to any mans right of dominion, or to the interest of men that have dominion, That the three Angles of a Triangle should be equall to two Angles of a Square; that doctrine should have been, if not disputed, yet by the burning of all books of Geometry, suppressed, as farre as he whom it concerned was able.*
>
> Hobbes, Leviathan

Plutarch narrates (1972, 607 F) that Anaxagoras, as a pass-time in prison, attempted to solve the problem of the quadrature of the circle. Some sustain that he was convinced to have found the exact solution (Hobson, 1913, p.14). Others raise doubts about Plutarch's story (Boyer, 1968, p.76). In any case, Plutarch was the first to describe a problem that has fascinated mathematicians for more than twentytwo centuries, before it was discovered that it was impossible to solve it according to the rules of Euclidean geometry, i.e. by using just a ruler and compass. The problem, roughly described, consisted of building a square with an area equivalent to that of a circle, i.e. in adjusting the circumference of the latter to obtain the same surface area enclosed within the figure. "But how did it all begin?" (Calasso, 1988, p.19). On this point only one thing is certain: that the problem of the quadrature of the circle, just like that of the other two of the "three famous classical problems" that go back to ancient times, i.e. duplication of the cube and trisection of an angle, implies the vague idea "that its solution would, in some dimly discerned manner, prove a key to a knowledge of the inner connections of things far beyond those with which the problem is immediately connected" (Hobson, 1913, p.4). The problem of cube duplication was posed by the oracle of Delphi, who advised the Athenians to double the altar to Apollo (a cube) to ward off the pest that was devastating the city. It may therefore be suggested that the quadrature of the circle was also a question whose solution was designed to fend off an appalling tragedy. But *why* did this all start? Anaxagoras was a friend of Pericles, in fact it was he who was closest to him (Plutarch, 1969, 4,6), and it was thanks to Pericles that he was released from prison. Another friend, or familiar acquaintance of Pericles was Herodotus, with whom the problem of geographical representation, what today we would call a map, was finally revealed for the first time in its true form: a matter of terror, anger and laughs. And it is precisely this story that helps to unveil the mystery of the quadrature of the circle.

Herodotus says (IV, 36): "For my part, I cannot but laugh when I see numbers of persons drawing maps of the world without having any reason to guide them; making, as they do, the ocean-stream to run all round the earth, and the earth itself to be an exact circle, as if described by a pair of compasses, with Europe and Asia just of the same size". What exactly is Herodotus laughing about here? Usually, it is thought that he is laughing at the excessive geometric nature of the geographic figures of his time, at the circular model of the Ionian *pinakes*, in short the subordination of the discourse, reasoning, logos to the drawing. The matter is however a bit more complicated. If Herodotus' real target was merely that just mentioned, his hilarity would appear to be very naive, or at least the result of a total loss of memory. If the opposite is true, it becomes much more malicious and intricate than first appears, and it is we who are naive in continuing to accept it at face value. In the sixth century BC. Anaximander created the first *pinax*, the first philosophical sculpture dedicated to the surface of the earth within the memory of Western civilisation. He used the same shape – recognized today – that characterized the epopea as a literary form and, more exactly. "the world of great literature from the classical epoch" (Bachtin, 1979, p.457, p.458, p.461): the circular form, that in the Homeric poems appears to be the product of the warrior practice of assembly, and from the assembly practice is transferred to the urban political space, to the *polis*. In the words of Jean-Pierre Vernant, one of the first to emphasize the close links between the reorganisation of the social space within the framework of a city and the reorganisation of the physical space in the new cosmological conceptions (analogous, it may be added, to geographic ones): "Now it must be observed that the political field also appears to be part of a spatial representation that deliberately places emphasis on the circle and the centre, giving them a well-defined meaning. In this respect it may be said that the advent of the city is marked first of all by the transformation of the urban space, i.e. the city plan. The plan of the new city appeared in the Greek world, and without doubt beforehand in the colonies, in which all the urban buildings were centred around a place or *agora*". In the "free debate that takes place in the centre of the *agora*, all the citizens define themselves as *isoi*, equals, *homoioi*, fellow-men. We witness the birth of a society in which the relationship between one man and another is viewed in the form of a relationship characterised by identity, symmetry, reversibility", equilibrium, reciprocity. This is stated even more clearly: "Despite the differences between them as regards residence, family, wealth, the citizens (or rather the houses) that make up a city-state form a political *koinonia* or *xynonie* due to their joint participation in this single space" (Vernant, 1970, p.210, p.212, p.219). The houses, we say, even before the inhabitants because the problem involves – as demonstrated by the Cleisthenian reform in the fifth century – the identification of the civic space with the territorial structure, the uniformity of which is strictly bound to the homogeneity of the former. In the fourth century, Plato gave a detailed description, in the *Laws* (745 b-e), of the result of this tension, the ideal model of "geometric equality" mentioned in *Gorgias* (507 e - 508 b), "omnipotent amongst the gods as amongst men": a circular city in which, around the acropolis, that was also circular, the land and the home of each individual citizen is arranged so that the mean of the two components is exactly the same distance from the centre as all the others. This model was already implicit in Anaximander's vision, whose recollected assembly origin makes it possible to establish the original social nature of the geometric scheme, that in Plato is presented as a secondary consideration, i.e. it is introduced at a subsequent moment and as the result of a calculated operation, as a technique for reaching a society project. In the case of Anaximander, social practice produces the formal model of knowledge, and at the same time the material model of the city. In the case of Plato, the circular model is applied to the description of a non-existent city, to the construction of a formal city model. In the first case the model is concrete and descriptive. In the second, abstract and prescriptive. To understand this reversal first of all it is necessary to reverse what P. Léveque and P. Vidal-Naquet (1964, p.13) claimed with regard to the birth of the civic space with Cleisthenes: that "the new realities can now be inscribed on a map". In my opinion the truth is the opposite: precisely because the map is now the *machina machinarum* of every reality, new realities and new ideas can now arise. In other words, and returning to the primordial model of the origins: it is not the *téchne*, that precisely at the time of Cleisthenes freed itself of all magic and religious elements (Vernant, 1970, p.318), that lies at the origin of the map, but rather is the *pinax* that is the origin of technology.

Léveque and Vidal-Naquet (1964, p.123) emphasize the coincidence between Anaximander's geometric vision of the universe and the "political vision of a rational and homogeneous city, like that of Cleisthenes", remarking how this solidarity disappeared during the fifth century. We, in turn, stress how Anaximander's model and Cleisthenes' isonomic conception, exactly like the maps that aroused Herodotus' hilarity and like the Ionian coins, were a circular shape. The problem still remains of the relationship between the two visions, that can be set out according to the scheme C-M-C', city-model(i.e. map)-city, that is:

Anaximander's *polis-pinax* that is modelled on the *polis*-Cleisthenes' *polis* that is modelled on Anaximander's *pinax*. In other words: Cleisthenes' concrete political construction derives, even before Plato's ideal one, from a model that is not concrete but is by its very nature abstract. The Cleisthenic *polis*, Athens at the end of the sixth century, was based on the equivalence, first established by Anaximander in the Greek world, between the world and (geometric, i.e. geographic) images of the world, to use Heidegger's language. And this was two thousand years before the epoch that the same Heidegger (1968, p.84) fixed for the birth of this same equivalence. The Cleisthenes' reform being the first, powerful manifestation of this, and the birth of the concept of political identity being the first formidable result of this manifestation. Prior to Cleisthenes, the citizen's identity derived primarily from his belonging to a *génos*, i.e. a race, or to a cult. With Cleisthenes, this depended mainly on belonging to a given territory and, at the same time, the recognition of the individual position within a plan, prior to this completely non-existent. As is explained very clearly by Christian Meier (1980, p.263): "A rupture occurred between social order and political order. The society, with all its inequalities, remained more or less the same. A new sphere sprang up alongside it – separate from it and with its own consolidated institutions – in which all were equal". He explains: "To be precise, it was not the state and society that were separated and concentrated in different circles of people. It was merely that, subsequently, there were two levels that co-existed, which no longer corresponded to one another in any way. The noble and the simple citizen (inasmuch as the latter were part of a united group) had a different influence at a political level to the social one. Thus eliminating the subordination arising from primarily social bonds". It is in fact only at a political level, within the political order, that a citizen, socially unequal to the others and who remains so, becomes, for the first time, the same as the others. But where does this ontological modification of ones position spring from, what is the nature of this equality, of this generalised (although not total) identity? Where does the new level, the new order come from, the birth of which according to Herodotus

(VI, 131) coincides with the advent of the democratic regime? How did this autonomy of the political sphere from the social reality come about? And, in the final analysis, where does democracy spring from?

To marvel that such crucial questions spring from reflections on what, in appearance, would seem to be a simple administrative reorganisation of the Athenian tribes is equivalent to admitting our fundamental naiveté as regards images that the majority of geographers still insist on considering as a mere means of expression, and not – as they should – as a powerful instrument for the production of conceptual figures and ways of thought: i.e. the cartographic image. On this matter, the Cleisthenic experience and its interpretation represent a model, at least for our culture. That the Cleisthenic reform, by its very nature, is based on the assumption of the use of a *pinax* is immediately evident, even if we have no documents on this. It consisted precisely in the redesigning of the Athenian administration according to the unheard-of principle of an order that was first and foremost spatial, i.e. it manifested itself in the first great and conscious experience of western territorial planning, perhaps not entirely unrelated – suggest Léveque and Vidal-Naquet (1964, p.68) – to the last wave of archaic colonisation. And there is no planning without a map, because spatial order can only arise from a map and this, with Anaximander, had already been conceived. Now, is exactly the nature of this order that transforms the administrative act into a political project, i.e. remodels not just the *forma urbis* but the nature of the relationship between the citizens, who assume the essence of perfectly equivalent geometric points. But this transformation is already implicit in the Anaximander model, where, as above mentioned, the circle gathering of soldiers joined in assembly, described by Homer, lends its shape to the universe, through the intermediate of the city form. As described by Karl Reinhardt (1960, p.256), with regard to Athenian citizenship: from a theoretical point of view it is equivalent to "a substance in which each amount, extracted at random from time to time, has the same structure and the same composition as the whole". This substance, that is equivalent to the political sphere and the reign of liberty, has got nothing to do with the dominion of necessity made up of a complex of social relations, but significantly overlaps it. Meier (1988, p.264) quotes on this point the expression of Hannah Arendt, according to whom everyday the Athenians had to cross an abyss when they went from home to the place, to the privileged area where the rights associated with citizenship were exercised.

Citizenship as a consequence, from Herodotus onwards, came to be known as *politeia*, the same term adopted to describe the constitution (Meier, 1988, p.307). Citizenship (i.e. political identity) and constitution thus became the same thing, and it is precisely this coincidence that takes us back, by analogy, to Anaximander. The isonomy implies first of all the fact that within the city the problem of power was no longer resolved by the presence of an arbiter, a foreign legislator, a tyrant – that is by a person – but through the functioning of the institutions. In this manner the person is replaced by an impersonal mechanism, a *nomos*, and as Carl Schmitt (1974, p.54) pointed out, before Plato *nomos* was a word with an original significance indissolubly linked to space, and meant "the first measurement, from which all the other measurement criteria are derived". To tell the truth, Schmitt claimed the strict derivation of the term from the occupation and division of the land, but this was clearly a meaning that had already been lost by the fifth century BC. Isonomy was, at least from the time of Cleisthenes onwards, a purely political notion, distinct from *isomoiria*, a word that at least since the time of Solon specifically indicated the division of land (Léveque and Vidal-Naquet, 1964, p.31). Thus, to justify Schmitt's reference, one is forced again to return to the map as the place in which it remained valid, which was at the same time the vehicle for transferring the significance of *nomos* to the field of abstract concepts: essential for its final transformation in the general legal, regulation or standard meaning in whatever manner presented or promulgated.

Isonomy and Anaximander's cosmic model are however strictly analogous, when not completely identical, and not just from a formal point of view. It is true that it was Thales, Anaximander's master, the inaugurator of the silent geometric *logos* (Colli, 1978, p.28), who advised unheeded the inhabitants of Ionia to use geometry to resolve the problems of the city (Léveque and Vidal-Naquet, 1964, p.66). But for Thales, again according to the traditional cosmology, the stability of the Earth was explained by the fact that it was sustained (and therefore depended on) by a different and external elementary force, by a kind of cushion of water. On the other hand, and for the first time, Anaximander explained the immobility of our planet on the basis of the purely geometric properties of space (Vernant, 1970, p.220). Thus, as in the case of isonomy, that which disappeared in the transition from the theory of the master to the theory of the pupil was the existence of a concrete substance (the equivalent of a living person in the case of the political regime) on which the cosmic order (the order of the city) is based. An order that now, in the case of the universe as in that of the *polis*, is no longer hierarchical but appears to be supported by an impersonal mechanism, by an identical and abstract logic: that of geometry and, precisely, of the constitution. And this occurs for the first time. On this point, Meier (1988, pp.301) offers an appropriate contribution. He explains how in the archaic *polis* – as far as can be established – equality derived from the fundamental homogeneity of the citizens, who were *homoiotes*, i.e. similar, being akin or alike from the qualitative point of view. At the other extreme, the isonomy that established itself in the fifth century is based on quantitative equality, as it describes "something that can be divided into absolutely equal parts, e.g. the shares of a booty". We will shortly see how in the century in question there was something very precious to be divided within the city itself.

In the meantime, let us return to Herodotus and his mirth: at this point we are able to understand it in its most secret meaning. It was noted that Anaximander's *pinax* and the isonomic city had the same form and follow the same logic: the logic that led Cleisthenes, at the end of the sixth century, to physically build "the first geometric city" (Léveque and Vidal-Naquet, 1964, p.78). Now, it is precisely against this circular Cleisthenic city of isonomy, homologous to the circular representation of the known world, that Herodotus was in fact, without saying, directing his irony. That is it concerned the regime of the polis, and not the image of the ecumene produced by this city. And this at the moment in which Herodotus, as already mentioned, cites Cleisthenes as the founder of democracy, i.e. precisely when he states the identical nature of isonomy and democracy. In reality, as pointed out by Léveque and Vidal-Naquet (1964, p.27) at a philological level, at the time of Cleisthenes the democratic idea, if it existed, was certainly not expressed with the term democracy, nor with any other similar term. It is therefore probable that Herodotus projects to the time of Cleisthenes, with a jump of more than half a century, the ideas and words belonging to the age of Pericles. And it may be suggested that, precisely due to his ideological interest in the demonstration of continuity (not just of lineage, but also political) between Pericles and his ancestor Cleisthenes, Herodotus ironizes not on the concrete and specific isonomic experience of the Athenians but on its more general and abstract expression, i.e. the circular map. What is however certain is that, as Thucydides vividly expresses himself (2, 65, 9) on Pericle's government, "it was called democracy, but in reality it was government by the first citizen". The significance of this expression can be appreciated even better if one notes, again guided by Léveque and Vidal-Naquet (1964, pp.28), that in the famous dialogue between the three Persian leaders during which Herodotus compares the merits and the drawbacks of the monarchy, the oligarchy and popular government, the defender of the democratic regime spoke as the representative of an epoch that did not recognise the difference between oligarchy and democracy, and in which isonomy merely signified opposition to tyranny. In other words the pretence of Herodotus is even more astute, because it concludes by presenting as identical two things that are historically and functionally opposite: the tyranny or semi-tyranny of Pericles and the isonomy of Cleisthenes, that Herodotus secretly ridicules. This, amongst other things, explains the insistence of the latter in defending the truth of his story against those who claimed that it was impossible for a Persian noble to defend democracy (Legrand, 1967, 108-9).

But there is another thing in the debate on the constitutions just quoted, a decisive phrase that in my opinion confirms everything said up until now, as well as explaining from the inside the reason why Herodotus selected this target for his sarcasm – a choice that in final analysis merely indicates the map as the matrix for all possible metaphors. "I deem that we give up the monarchy and raise the multitude to power (*to pléthos*); in fact it is in the multitude (or in the greatest number: *to pollo*) that everything lies (*ta panta*)": thus Otane, the supporter of the isonomic ideal, concludes his discourse (Herodotus, III, 80). *En gar to pollo éni ta panta*: the last, lapidary expression creating considerable problems, and being translated in many different ways. Meier (1988, p.295) confesses that he had still not managed to disentangle the literal translation, that according to him reads: "in the majority in fact everything is contained". And adds however that the majority principle is also in force in oligarchies, and therefore the reference here is not to this. I think however that first of all the important thing is the relationship between the noun and the adjective used as a noun, between *to pléthos* and *to polù*: the first case without doubt refers to the majority of citizens, there is therefore the reference to the concrete civic universe; the second passes to an abstract realm, reference is made to a principle that today would be defined as theoretical, that is used as the foundation and justification of the empirical choice just expressed. In this way passing from the particular to the general. The decisive mutation is however the following, i.e. that which leads from *to polù* to *ta panta*, in the course of which the foundation of the foundation is realised, the justification of the justification, because the transfer is produced from the field of the existing, of beings and phenomena, to that of the nature of Being and its categories. But where does the nature of Being reduce itself in a primorbial manner to the being to the extent of being contained within it, if not in the geographic image, the map? In what other place, on which other occasion does that which appears take on in an archetypal manner the place of that which *is*? One could also say with the language of Anaximander: where the "things" become "things-that-are" (Colli, 1978, p.155), and we can therefore come to know them and manipulate them? It is precisely in this translation, in this reduction, that we have the primigenial function of that which today we call cartographic representation: primigenial because it is precisely from this act that according to Anaximander it is possible to have order in the world, and for Cleisthenes in the city. Perhaps my interpretation is only supported by the knowledge that "an advance is only decisive when it unveils, at the moment in which it is raised, the primitive archaisms" (Serres, 1993, p.27). But if my interpretation is correct, Otane, drawing on the final consequences of the isonomic principle and thus illustrating it in detail, says: for everything (the "thing": *to panta*) to be reduced to multitude, becoming ontic multitude (the "thing-that-is": *to polù*), this must also be applicable to urban government, for the power, that then coincides with the multitude of visible signs (geometric points), with the *plethos*, with the totality of citizens. Which at the same time is nothing more than the simulacrum of a simulacrum, exactly as for Anaximander the distance between sign and reality is not single but double (Farinelli, 1988, pp.8). Applying the urban model to the entire known world and to the entire universe, Anaximander did not just formalise it but he generalised it. And it is precisely merely on the basis of this generalisation that the geometric form can become a principle that constitutes and regulates the universe. From this point of view the first map becomes a real laboratory, within which we have the first crucial transformation: just as in the *pinax* the world changes into signs, what is ontological changes, passing through the ontic, into phenomenal, and the categorical force released in this manner becomes literally abstract, thus capable of reinvesting in an impersonal manner, in such a way as to escape the awareness of any human being, reality as a whole, surreptitiously redefining the nature of everything. This is why Cleisthenes' reform is based on the assumption of Anaximander's hubris, and would be impossible without it – this is why Cleisthenes' administrative act becomes political, becomes the foundation of the Political.

Not even Herodotus' thought, despite his irony, can escape from the cartographic determination that begins here. To sum up, his laugh was merely aimed at replacing one cartographic form with another, the circular with the tetragonal, as the image of the world. The circular profile survived well beyond the time when it was fully understood that the ecumene was greater in lenght (west to east) than in breadth (south to north) (Aujac, 1987, p.135). But this was because cosmography always wins over topography, in the sense that it always lasts longer. In fact all the maps used by Herodotus for his *History* are quadrangular, built on the basis of a linear axis that coincides with a communication route (Myres, 1986, p.628). To understand the reason we must now introduce, after Anaximander and Herodotus, another friend of Pericles, Hippodamus from Miletus, the first great urban architect of the Greek world but also the first political theorist in the true sense. His name is remembered today mainly because he was the author, or more exactly the codifier, of the orthogonal urban plan, with the roads crossing one another at right-angles precisely within a quadrangular space. And it is no mere chance that Herodotus, born in point of fact at Halicarnassus, proudly proclaims in the first line of his work that he is a citizen of Thurii, the pan-Hellenic colony apparently designed precisely by Hippodamus and whose foundation, in 444/3 BC, marked the completion of the Athenian political horizon, the bond between eastern and western Greeks. And the fact takes on an even greater significance if one remembers that the policy of Pericles was no longer just that based on mere territorial expansion, but at the same time was based on the spreading of "an ideological approach that tends to identify the vision of a Greek way of life, i.e. *hellenikòn*, with that of the Athenians" (Nenci, 1979, pp.45), i.e. based on the exportation and imposition of exemplary models – probably starting from the urban model. In short, Thurii was how the Athens of Pericles should have been, it was the *Idealtypus*, or came as close as possible to this. And its quadrangular form, unlike that of Athens, free of any historic ties and any past urban heritage, was precisely that of the new geographic representations, the new maps: Thurii was a city which embodied the new image of the world, functional to Athenian imperialism and to its project of creating a great trading area, a great common market within which even the antithesis between Greek and barbarian disappeared. As described by another friend of Pericles, Antiphon, who asserted: "*by nature* we are all equal (*homoioi*), foreigners and Greeks" (Diels-Kranz, 1954, pp.352: my underlining).

This affirmation is important because it records with extreme clarity the passage from the Cleisthenes' civic space, still differentiated from a qualitative point of view (Léveque and Vidal-Naquet, 1964, p.77), to the space that is qualitatively undifferentiated, but merely quantitatively distinct, that is in fact the result of the inversion that is now established between urban form and *pinax*. In the case of Anaximander it is the second that depends, as has been shown, on the first, and isonomy is the product of this dependence. The democracy of Pericles is therefore the consequence of the reversing of this relationship, i.e. of the independence of the cartographic image with respect to the urban reality, that now, furthermore, takes on the same figure of the image used to depict it. Exactly as Léveque and Vidal-Naquet (1964, p.133) assert: the new vision of political order, from Hippodamus to Plato, is no longer founded "on the city itself, but precisely on the world order". Correct. But only if "world" is used to mean map, and if we understand that the map has definitely replaced the world and governs it with its own logic of quantitative equivalence, that the identity between world and map has implacably changed to the dominion of the map over the world. And the city is no longer, as in the case of isonomy, the starting point but the result of this order, it does not produce it but is subject to it, in the form of democracy.

To comprehend the consequences, we will now go to the place, in the centre of the city. It was Borges (1985, p.1341) who poetically explained the function of the place, imagining two Greeks who, forgetting prayer and magic, putting aside myth and metaphor, converse and "try to think", and are in agreement on one point: that "discussion is the not impossible path to reach the truth". But it was Gottlob Frege, without meaning to, who technically explained the nature of this discussion. Frege's problem (1971, pp.102) consisted in determining whether the proposition $a = b$ could contain real elements of knowledge. Thus he wrote: "Given a, b, c, the straight lines drawn from the vertices of a triangle to the centre of the opposite sides. The point of intersection of a with b is the same as the point of intersection of b with c. We have different names for the same point and these names ('point of intersection of a with b', 'point of intersection of b with c') indicate at the same time the manner in which this point was arrived at". Thus, concludes Frege, to say that a = b, that the evening star is the morning star, corresponds to the effective knowledge of something, since, although they refer to the same object, although they indicate the same celestial body, a and b express two different approaches, two of its different senses. As also explained by Olsson (1980, p.47b), returning to the language of Russell: the proposition is true and informative, because "the morning star" and the "evening star" are two definite descriptions that indicate the same heavenly body. In other words, and returning to the language of Frege: knowledge is only possible as a result of the difference between *Sinn* and *Bedeutung*, between sense and reference or meaning. But this difference presupposes a material centre (Fig. 1), the *agorà*, involves a concrete act, that of debate, assumes a determinate form, that of dialectics, and produces something very precious, information.

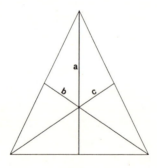

Figure 1

In the case of the circular city (Fig. 2) the senses are infinite, and the sense vectors, i.e. the diameters whose lines correspond to the ideal path of the citizens, are absolutely identical to one another. It is true that the distance between two points (two citizens) increases as one moves from the centre towards the circumference – and presumably precisely for this reason Plato devised the model mentioned above. The decisive factor remains however that, with regard to the centre, that is the public space, this distance remains absolutely identical for both: and this is the best illustration of what should be understood by isonomy. In the case of the quadrangular Hippodamian city (Fig. 3) the relationship between centre and citizens, and between citizen and citizen, is on the other hand the opposite to the previous ones. The vectors are unlike one another because they have three different lengths, and this is because the distance between the individual citizens and the centre is programmatically different. As a consequence, however, it always remains identical between them, regardless of the distance from the centre. In this way we have an authentic opposition: within the circular city the civic distance is *equal from the centre, unequal between citizens*; within the quadrangular city it is, exactly the opposite, *equal between the citizens, unequal from the centre*. It is precisely in this inversion that we have the passage from isonomy to democracy.

The main advantage of this inversion, in fact the only one, is the speed with which information is circulated, that within the Hippodamian scheme is obviously, precisely as a result of the equal

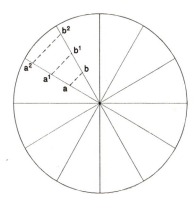

Figure 2

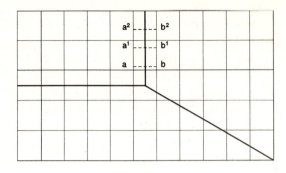

Figure 3

civic distance, much faster than within the Cleisthenic polis. Faster but programmatically it is also unequal and therefore in the final analysis selective, due to the original and systematic interval inherent in the relationship with the centre, in the structural dissimilarity in the position of the same citizens. Thus, in the light of the above, an attempt can also be made to formulate a definition of democracy as a regime that attempts to reconcile the isonomic ideal with the speed of the circulation of information, on the basis of the principle of the rectilinear calculation of the distances within the city and the known world – the same principle that, with the Latin name *celeritas*, began the reduction of western space to the time taken to cover the same space (Rambaud, 1974), and from a war strategy became in modern times a criterion for the construction of every economic strategy. Strategy that first appears in the Hippodamian city, and whose victory is announced precisely by Herodotus' laugh. As was declared around the middle of the first century B. C. by the stoic Geminus (1975, 16,5): "beware of the distances marked on round maps because the ecumene cannot be circumscribed by a circle, since it is a portion of a sphere whose length is twice that of the width". In other words: the unforgivable defect of circular maps lies in the fact that the further one moves from the centre, the greater the relative distance between two points (the first piece of information necessary to set up a functional market) is distorted.

However, already in 434 Turi no longer recognized Athens as metropolis, mother-state, and this is perhaps the final indication of the imminent end of Pericles' dream, of the crisis in his highly ambitious because contradictory project: export though power politics a government formula based on the more radical and direct democracy. The quadrature of the circle cannot be achieved, and this must be taken literally: isonomy (the first historical form of equality of all citizens before the law) is based, even before reciprocal similarity and absence of domination, on an authentic and material centrality, and therefore absolute respect of the circular form. Thus the crisis of the more or less pacific Athenian imperialism is already inherent in the Hippodamian plan: a formidable example of how *diorthosis*, rectification, is an operation that does not merely involve the shape but above all the nature of things, for which it establishes the ontological statute and the functioning methods even before the correct image. It is through this that the Earth becomes a copy of the map. Thus Baudrillard (1981, p. 10) is completely wrong when he restricts the "precession of simulacra" to the post-modern condition: this began precisely with Herodotus' laugh. It is like saying that the crisis of Pericles is still ours, because the conciliation between equality before the law and market functioning is still our problem: precisely the same problem that Anaxagoras, in prison, tried to resolve attempting the impossible transformation of a circle (of a city, of a circular world) into a square.

References

Aujac G, 1987 "The Foundations of Theoretical Cartography in Archaic and Classical Grece", in *The history of Cartography, I, Cartography in Prehistoric, Ancient, and Medieval Europe and Mediterranean* Eds J.B. Harley, D. Woodward (The University of Chicago Press, Chicago and London) pp 130-47

Bachtin M, 1979 "Epos e romanzo", in *Estetica e romanzo* (Einaudi, Torino) pp 445-82

Baudrillard J, 1981 *Simulacres et simulation* (Galilée, Paris)

Borges J, 1985 "Atlante" in *Tutte le opere*, II (Mondadori, Milano) pp 1309-1423

Boyer C B, 1976 *Storia della matematica* (Mondadori, Milano)

Calasso R, 1988 *Le nozze di Cadmo e Armonia* (Adelphi, Milano)

Colli G, 1978 *La sapienza greca*, II (Adelphi, Milano)

Diels H, Kranz W, 1954 *Die Fragmente der Vorsokratiker*, II (Weidmann'sche Verlagsbuchhandlung, Berlin)

Farinelli F, 1989 *Pour une théorie générale de la géographie* (Departement de Géographie, Universite de Genève)

Frege G, 1971 "Sens et dénotation" in *Ecrits logiques et philosophiques* (Seuil, Paris) pp 102-26

Geminus, 1975 *Introduction aux Phénomenes* (Les Belles Lettres, Paris)

Heidegger M, 1968 "L'epoca dell'immagine del mondo", in *Sentieri interrotti* (La Nuova Italia, Firenze) pp 78-112

Hérodote, 1967 *Histoires*, III (Les Belles Lettres, Paris)

Hobson E W, 1913 *"Squaring the Circle". A History of the Problem* (University Press, Cambridge)

Legrand Ph E, 1967 "Notice" in Hérodote, *Histoires*, III (Les Belles Lettres, Paris) pp 91-119

Léveque P, Vidal-Naquet P, 1964 *Clisthène l'Athénien* (Macula, Besançon)

Meier Ch, 1988 *La nascita della categoria del politico in Grecia* (Il Mulino, Bologna)

Myres J L, 1986 "An Attempt to Reconstruct the Maps Used by Herodotus" *The Geographical Journal* 7 (2) pp 605-29

Nenci G, 1979 "Formazione e carattere dell'impero ateniese" in *Storia e civiltà dei Greci, 3, La Grecia nell'età di Pericle* Ed R. Bianchi Bandinelli (Bompiani, Milano)

Olsson G, 1980 *Birds in Egg/Eggs in Bird* (Pion, London)

Platon, 1965 *Lois*, III (Les Belles Lettres, Paris)

Platon, 1968 *Gorgias* (Les Belles Lettres, Paris)

Plutarcus, 1972 *De exilio* (Teubner, Leipzig)

Plutarch, *Life of Pericles* (Loeb, London-Cambridge MA)

Rambaud M, 1969"L'espace dans le récit césarien" in *Mélanges offerts à Roger Dion* Ed R. Chevallier (Picard, Paris)

Reinhardt K, 1960 *Tradition und Geist* (Vandenhoeck und Ruprecht, Göttingen)

Schmitt C, 1991 *Il nomos della Terra* (Adelphi, Milano)

Serres M, 1993 *Les origines de la géométrie* (Flammarion, Paris)

Thucydides, 1956 *History of the Peloponnesian War* (Loeb, London-Cambridge MA)

Vernant J-P, 1970 *Mito e pensiero presso i Greci* (Einaudi, Torino)

CHIASM OF THOUGHT-AND-ACTION

by Gunnar Olsson

There is a double helix in the social sciences too, a chiasm of thought-and-action, an epistemological braiding of ontological antinomies, an imagination of what it is to be human. Life is form, form the modality of life.

I prefer the term "imagination" to that of "theory", for in my experience every theory carries within it a trace of commission, an (un)conscious adjustment to a particular interest, an attitude that it is not enough to understand the world, but that I must change it as well. Built into the theoretical is in fact a hostility to abstractness, a temptation to thingification, a utilitarian shift from social science to social engineering. "Can" turns to "ought", opportunity to obligation, possibility to necessity. Court painters nevertheless lead the dangerous lives they deserve, for their masters hate ingratiation as much as humility, integrity as much as laughter. Social realism is bad art for the same reasons that social engineering is bad ethics, less because knowledge is power, more because power is knowledge. Ass-lickers become ball-biters, castrated eunuchs.

My own imagination has emerged gradually, in stages without breaks. Thus there are clear affinities between my current concerns and the etchings of *Birds in Egg/Eggs in Bird*, the watercolors of *Antipasti*, and the oils of *Lines of Power/Limits of Language*. How do I know the difference between you and me and how do we share our beliefs in the same? To which extent is it I who speak through language and language that speaks through me? How are we made so obedient and so predictable?

*

If only I could know others, then others could know me. Impossible, for just as the "now-here" of time and space is a linguistic shifter, so is the "I" of personal identity. Once caught in the cultural net of à priori categories, the I does not know whether it is itself or one of its too many duplicates. Since the image in the mirror simultaneously re-flects reality and in-forms the ego, a man cannot get rid of the relation to himself any more than he can get rid of himself. The logical, the moral, the aesthetic are analogous, for all are self-referential. It is in deed in the proper name of Kant itself that his critiques must be taken to their limits. But a limit can never be understood, for understanding is itself a limit.

Such is the desire of my imagination: a minimalist rendering of how we define ourselves, an acknowledgement that linguistic signs are forms *of* art shaped by forms *in* art. Like Piet Mondrian and Samuel Beckett I therefore dream of a work in which "the expression of things gives way to the pure expression of relation", where my writing is "not *about* something, [but] *is* that something itself". Preliminary sketches have appeared before, first under the heading "Malevic sfigurato", then as the two chapters "Squaring" and "Malevich Torpedoed", most recently in the tourist brochure "Invisible Maps". If desire is mimetic, how do I draw the likeness of Nothingness?

* * * * *

Common to my various sketches are two assumptions. One is that man is a semiotic animal, a species whose individuals are kept together and apart by their use of signs, the other that every sign within itself combines elements of drastically different ontologies. The latter stem from the legacy of Descartes, even though their specific names vary with the contexts in which they occur; sometimes they are called use value and exchange value, sometimes sense and reference, mind and matter, presence and absence, signifier and signified. Oversimplified, one part of the antinomic pairs is in the physicality or corporeality of the sign, the other in the intentionality of its cultural meaning. The former is open to the five senses, the latter to the sixth. And yet it is important to recall not only that every thought occurs to a flesh but also that there can be no art without matter; poetry is written with words, not with ideas, paintings are painted with paint, not with concepts.

Partly for the sake of the French, mainly for that of analysis, it is necessary to distinguish between signifier, S, and signified, s. Talk about things and relations belong to different language games. It must nevertheless be remembered that every sign within itself contains both ingredients at the same time. *Mens sana in corpore sano.*

Like the eye of anatomy, also the I of the sign can both see and be seen. In neither case, however, is what and how I see independent of the particular world I am a part of. It is in this double sense (of the distinctive correspondence between outside and inside, inside and outside) that the carnal being is the prototype of Being-in-the-world. I hear myself not through my ears but through my tongue. I see myself not through my eyes but through my touch. I eat what I am. Therefore, whenever in doubt, always trust your body, for body is biological matter and cultural mind intertwined.

My body is neither thing nor idea, but the measure of a thing. And thus it is that even when a woman talks, I can never fully understand her. Lips are lips, kisses are kisses. The marble of the sculpture is not the marble of the quarry, the gold on the finger not the gold in the bank. Yet you know what it means to miss New Orleans. A rose is a rose is a symbol of love.

*

Just as the body carries the initiation scars of circumcision, pierced ears, and tattooed chests, so does the mind. Thus, the normal psyche is marked by its ability to draw and to symbolize real distinctions, by its unconscious memories of the imaginary. Understanding the difference between you and me is in practice to live a split life without going crazy. In contrast, the psychotic neither makes nor shares distinctions, for in the Land of Psychosis there are no initiation rites, no marks, nothing social. The loss of not knowing the loss of inclusion is an echoless scream in a mountainless valley. In the words of Jean-Jacques Rousseau's *Heloise*: "Wanting to be what we are not, we come to believe ourselves something other than what we are, and this is how we get mad".

It follows that any scar is better than no scar, for without exclusion and inclusion nothing exists, not even nothing. 'And that, Herr

Goldschmidt, that is why you must submit, when I now execute the will of my Führer. Bitte, pull down your pants! Prove with your cock who you are, just as the beriddled Oedipus once did with his swollen foot. What does your name mean, Herr Goldschmidt? Was it not your Lord who declared that the cut in the flesh of your foreskin is a sign of the covenant between Him and you?'

Alas for the seed of men. Identity as sameness and difference brought together. Parricide and incest as transgressions of the sacred boundary between man and beast. The tragic hero as violator of the limits he himself has established, victim of his own words, law maker as law breaker. How come that we are so obedient and predictable that when someone points it out we feel uncomfortable? Titian's *Flaying of Marsyas* is the most gruesome of paintings, the Holocaust the most unmentionable of acts.

*

And so it is that every sign carries an invisible mark of distinction, itself visualized in the line of

$$\frac{S}{s} \text{ and } \frac{s}{S}$$

I would even go so far as to suggest that every sign can be condensed into the dash of the fraction line. This is not to say, however, that my minimalism is a reductionism, only that there is a fundamental narcissism in all vision, hence in all thought-and-action. Put differently, even though S and s are obsessed by a desire to be the same, that desire can never be satisfied. It follows that the semiotic animal is thoroughly paradoxical, for it can be what it is only by being what it is not.

One reason is that meaning does not reveal itself in the identities intended, but in the differences achieved. Another is that immediately I write

$$\frac{S}{s} \text{ or } \frac{s}{S}$$

then the signified ceases to be a pure signified and turns into a signifier. In my own conception, the fraction line serves as a symbol of the real castration that bears the transmission of culture. Perhaps the bar is the trace of the real, for it is exactly here that the five senses touch the sixth. Desire is not the desired, desire is desire. Desire is not the meaning of the meaning of the upper- or lower-case s, desire is the invisible —. The semiotic animal wants nothing. All it asks is to be believed, all it needs is response. Desire is the desire of having one's desire recognized.

Not *Desidero ergo sum*, but *Desiderare ergo sum*. Not that "*I* desire therefore I am", but that "*Desire* therefore I am". Human beings lend signification to everything, especially and foremost to their thoughts-and-actions. Seducer seduced. Tracers tracing traces tracing tracers. Fox-hounds. Sour grapes.

* * *

Put together, the two assumptions of man as a semiotic creature and the sign as a fraction lead to a conception of thought-and-action as a play of ontological transformations. Whenever he thinks and-acts, man is a juggler of Cartesian categories, one torch in his hand the other in the air. The ruling paradigm remains that of the *Genesis*: "Let there be! – And there was."

In performing its speech acts, the Word becomes flesh and dwells among us, full of grace and truth and honey-sucking bees. Socialization writ large, creativity as the art of making the present absent, the absent present. And yet it is in the brutality of facts that reality shows itself less in copies of the external, more in gestures of the unconscious. Thus, I once again catch a glimpse of that Hopper woman in the airport lounge, blue dress, one leg on top of the other. The angle of her knee returns my glance, thereby confirming that I exist. And then in the coolness of the evening I thought well as well her as another and then I asked her with my eyes to ask again yes and would I yes to say yes my mountain flower. The keys to. Given!

To exercise power is in this perspective to perform the double trick of turning things into relations, relations into things, inner into outer, outer into inner. And as a way of illuminating its own function, the word "image" carries connotations not only of "phantom" but also of "statue", not only of fantasy but also of *Homo erectus* –

Phallus of the phallus.

It cannot be said more clearly: the world of thought-and-action is bat-like. Viewed from one direction it looks like a bird, from another like a mouse. No wonder that power is so poorly understood, for already the *Leviticus* classified the bat among the unclean. To be unclean is by definition to be a member of the class of the non-classifiable, to be neither this nor that, neither fish nor fowl. To be in the taboo is to be in a limit. In-between is an abyss, the bottomless pit of primal chaos. The American savages were taught the Spanish grammar, for without grammar the Conquistadores could never conquer.

*

For the conventional theorist, ambiguity presents an insurmountable obstacle. Unclean is the hare because it chews the cud but does not part the hoof, unclean the swine because it parts the hoof but does not chew the cud, unscientific the study whose subject matter hops capriciously about. Without order no knowledge, without knowledge no power.

In my own imagination, the ambiguous order of thought-and-action can be condensed into a dematerialized point. This origo of abstractness is itself a version of Wassily Kandinsky's geometric point. In its minimalism it belongs to language and signifies silence. In its stillness it belongs to contemplation and signifies change. Graphically:

*

To bring the silence of these lines into common parlance, they must be properly baptized. I therefore now name the vertical axis "IDENTITY" and the horizontal "DIFFERENCE". Both are nevertheless silent lines, the former white and cold, the latter black and warm. In the origo is the muteness of the taken-for-granted, hence the orthogonality of the coordinate net. It follows that before a line can break into speech it must be tilted; for Piet Mondrian – prime investigator of silence – the diagonal was so full of deceit that when Theo van Doesburg began to paint it, their friendship was over. While the classicism of modernism accepts the frame, the baroque of postmodernism tries to break it.

At the end-points of the two axes lie extreme forms of silence. These extremes can themselves be given specific names, and it is on your acceptance of them that the credibility of my imagination eventually hinges. In a sense, they represent special cases of the sign and thereby the fix-points of thought. More specifically:

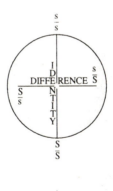

*

It is obvious from this drawing that I imagine thought simultaneously as the telescope of my rifle and the deer of my hunt. At the empty center of the cross lies the dematerialized point with which I aim at the world; at the periphery is the ring that represents the limit of language, hence of thought. The end-points of the horizontal line touch this limit from the inside, those of the vertical mark it from the outside. Moving the rifle up and down, I capture the world in its metaphoric likeness, moving it sideways, I trace the displacements of the metonymic. To capture is to metaphorize, to trace is to metonymize.

Roman Jacobson's analyses of aphasia come readily to mind. But so does also the image of Diana's bath, important both to Titian and to Jacques Lacan. You remember the story: Diana has been hunting the whole day. She is warm and when she comes upon a stream of water she strips bare and wades into it. But behind a bush hides Actaeon in his spying caught by Diana's eye. Trouble in the making, for possessed she will no longer be the unpossessed virgin that drives gods and mortals mad, unseen she will not be THE woman Actaeon imagines. Perhaps that is why the voyeur had to be turned into a stag, pursued and eventually killed by his fifty hounds. Huntress hunted, desire as lack, lack as desire. To desire is in essence to metonymize, to realize that to desire is not to have an object but to be a subject. Yet there can be no desire without embodiment, no sucking without breasts. To be human is to be mammalian.

Thus there is an erotic in every truth, for "truth" is itself a mode of socialization. And as if to prove its own point, this particular essay is threatening less because of its doctrines, more because of its passions. See what I mean. Sucker!

Exaggerating? Of course! How else could I understand? How else could I convince? Not that she shouldn't, not that she wouldn't, and I know it's not that she couldn't. It's simply because she's the laziest gal in town.

*

It is in this same vein of understanding and convincing that I associate the ring of my telescope with the final paragraph of Ludwig Wittgenstein's *Tractatus*. The reason is that after Plato understanding is geometric and communication phallogocentric; here nobody enters who does not know his geometry. It follows first that of what one cannot see, thereof one cannot speak, and then that "whereof one cannot speak, thereof one must be silent". In actuality, I see not with my I's eye but with my pupil, not with my pupil but with my brain, not with my brain but with my mind. The world is a fantasy, an imaginary construction of the mind.

Thus it is with my mind's eye that I can sense how the two endpoints of the identity axis reach toward the outside limit of language. Properly speaking, these two points cannot be named, for they are devoid of difference. At one extreme is the

$$\frac{s}{s}$$

which is the imagined sign of pure spirit, at the other the

$$\frac{S}{S}$$

the imagined sign of pure matter. The former is in the ether that clouds the top of Olympus, the latter in the rocks that strew the shores of Scylla and Carybdis.

The allusions to mythology prompt themselves, for at least since antiquity man has tried to define who he is. This has led him into fighting a kind of two-front war, where one enemy is that of pure spirituality the other that of pure physicality. Put differently, one boundary dispute concerns the difference between man and god, the other the distinction between man and beast. In the former No-Man's Land threatens the hubris of the superhuman, in the latter the degradation of the subhuman. In between is the imaginary of the human itself, for only man knows how to imagine. What turns Oedipus Tyrannos into a tragic figure is that he oscillates between being the equal of gods and being the equal of nothing at all. His sin is that he is a slayer of distinctions, father and son in one, husband of his mother, child of his wife. Identity is never indifferent, for certainty rules in a world of ambiguity. Cloven foot, rabbi run.

The front-lines move back and forth. To illustrate, the Greeks prior to the fifth century did not even possess a word for "human will", for to them a man could not act on his own, only as an instrument of the gods. In addition, gods were condemned to eternal life and that is why no Greek ever wanted to be one of them. But then, two and a half millennia later, Friedrich Nietzsche could define the human as the will to power. God is dead, Man is god! Proud rulers are no longer descendants sent from Heaven, but representatives of the Electorate; *l'État c'est moi*, the Whip of self-reference.

In the meantime, the other front-line has fluctuated too. While for the Greeks women and slaves were not really human, current issues in ethics involve such matters as the rights of animals and fertilized eggs. This is in essence what Environmentalism is about: the limit between the beastly and the human, the cloven hoofs and the silken paws.

Whether the total territory of the imaginary has increased or decreased is a moot question. Some would argue that man has invaded the Land of Gods, others that idiots have peopled the Land of Man. Perhaps it is the gods of television that today govern mankind, perhaps the engineers of thought that command atoms and genes. *Das also war des Pudels Kern,* the inevitability of the Faustian pact, the conflict between the Word of the Old Testament and the Deed of the New. Beware of your soul! Not everything is for sale.

On our way from dust to dust, the questions remain the same: Who am I and which is the difference between you and me? In contrast, the answers keep changing, for answers are always contextual. In the utopian No-where of now-here they point to the political ideologies of the twentieth century, to paradox and predicament, to intentionality caught by the tail of its own tale.

Such is the current price of being obedient, for such is the speech of silence: *Beyond* the limits of language. Babble's wall from the outside.

*

The signs at the end-points of the identity axis are silent, because their nominator and denominator are the same, their fraction equal to one. The crossing of the bar has gone unnoticed, the circumcission leaving not a scar of proof. The end-points of the difference axis are silent as well, but here it is because the signifier and the signified are too different to be connected. This is typical of what I elsewhere have called the "crisis of the sign", the experience that there are no words for what I really feel, no political representatives of who I really am.

Also the signs of difference take two extreme forms, viz.

$$\frac{S}{s}$$

and

$$\frac{s}{S}$$

The first denotes an expression in search of its meaning, the second an intention in search of its expression. The former is the sign à la Jacques Lacan, the latter à la Ferdinand de Saussure. The arts of surrealism and postmodernism are in the first mood, the politics of nazism, communism and social democracy in the second.

The survival rates of these ideologies seem inversely proportional to their degree of inhumanity. For that reason, I am eternally grateful to the Fate that in 1935 let me born in Sweden and not in Germany or the Soviet Union. But this happy circumstance must not keep me from understanding that everything has a price, also the politics of the welfare state. How do I insult a power which is so powerful that it is faceless? How do I learn about difference, when difference is defined away? How do I topple a regime which has no statues erected in its honor? How do I find my way in a jungle of paragraphs? In short: How can I live in a culture which is so proud of its penis that it is unaware of its Phallus? Why is it so hard to detect the difference between the "*Nom-du-Père*" and the "*Non-du-Père*"?

Perhaps there is in these questions yet another connection with the rhetorical tropes of metaphor and metonymy. Thus, whereas metaphor is what is said and shown, metonymy is what is heard and seen. What I give is a metaphor, what you receive is a metonymy. Metaphor is the spark, metonymy the explosive. The metaphor of metaphors is the anchor, the metaphor of metonymies the arrow. By saying how things are, I show who I am. I speak less for the purpose of informing, more for speaking the speaking.

It is in this double sense of holding fast and letting loose that both knowledge and power are structured as a language. While the conscious focuses on the metaphoric of the sign's nominator, the unconscious hides in its denominator. The locus of power is nevertheless in the invisibility of the fraction line, in the simultaneous separation and joining of the S and the s, the s and the S. Emperor on the balcony, child in the gutter. Spiders in the bedrooms of the Kakanian castles.

Such is the silence of speech: *Within* the limits of language. Babble's wall from the inside.

* * *

Thus is my imagined vision of the plane of thought: a cross centered on a dematerialized point and surrounded by a halo of silence. Where is the action?

The action is in another dimension, captured by a third axis. This line, which I hereby name "INTENTIONALITY" or, more properly, "DESIRE", passes through the dematerialized point at a right angle. Graphically:

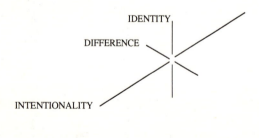

*

Also the end-points of the intentionality axis can be named, and also here the variation is in terms of thinghood. At one extreme, desire is totally thingified, at the other completely spiritualized. In the former case, the signifier is most properly written as $\underline{S}$, in the latter as $\check{s}$. My wording indicates that I see action less from the ethical viewpoint of intentions and more from the psychoanalytic standpoint of the unconscious; while intentions serve as colonizing projections into the future, the unconscious is the memory of the forgotten. In certain circumstances nothing is more noticeable than a lack of purpose.

What I denote by s̄ comes close to the concept of the sublime, that which stems from the *sub limis*, i.e. that which is uplifted from under the threshold. To feel the sublime is to experience how imagination approaches its own limits, for sublimation does not represent the thing lost but actually recreates it. In painting, the sublime is that which remains invisible, in chemistry sublimation is the conversion of a substance from the solid to the vapour state without its being liquid in between.

In contrast, the S̲ comes closer to the repressed. In Freudian terms, the individual who is perfectly repressed is also perfectly socialized. In Lacan's world, on the other hand, repression is less an issue of forgetting desire and more of speaking the truth. Since truth by definition is unspeakable, repression constitutes the paradoxical "representation" of the ultimate silence of death. René Girard's theory of mimetic desire and the killing of the double comes to mind as well, for it is when desire momentarily reduces itself to the scapegoat of need that it effectively guarantees its own perpetuation. It is in this sense that desire reveals itself through its own negation; the dialectics of desire is a dialectics of signification, of making a thing present by its absence.

In normal situations, both sublimation and repression are part of the defense mechanisms without which anybody would go crazy. Carried to their ultimate consequences, however, they reach toward silence and thereby madness. To distinguish these cases, I denote the SUBLIME and the REPRESSED of madness with the letters s and S, and the sublime and repressed of normalcy with the barred notation s̄ and S̲. The former touch the limits of language from the outside, the latter from the inside.

Finally, it should be noted explicitly that the axis of intentionality cuts through the plane of thought at the dematerialized point of the equal sign. It is in this same point that action appears in its most purified form, farthest away from the extremes of both s̄ and S̲. Here, as in the aufgehoben state of the man without qualities, nothing stirs in her now, not even her splendid desire. It is through this point that all thought-and-action must pass, for it is in this point that everything turns to its opposite.

*

When turned around the intentionality axis, the coordinate system forms a three-dimensional volume shaped like an American football. It is this suspended figure that in my imagination offers the most abstract picture of thought-and-action:

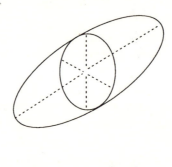

* * * * *

Thus is the form of my imagination: black marks projected onto a screen of white paper. The Name-of-the-Father performing its double functions of law and order, legislation and punishment.

And just as Carl von Linné could build his classificatory system on observations of stamina and pistils, so I now think of the concepts of signifier and signified as serving similar functions in the realm of thought and language. And just as the boiling and freezing of water led Anders Celsius to the design of his thermometer, so I dream of the various forms of silence as fix-points in a set of maps from the Land of Action. The territory to be explored is like America between Cristóbel Colón and Amerigo Vespucci; unknown to the white Spaniards, familiar to the red Indians. Stanley, stay home! Mother Matrix rules.

In actuality, the signs of thought-and-action seldom occur in the clearcut forms of the proposed structure. Instead they show themselves at various stages of imbalance; sometimes the signifier is more prominent, sometimes the signified, sometimes the sublime, sometimes the repressed. The most immediate task is therefore to discover, name and order a set of illustrative cases. It must nevertheless be borne in mind that it is through abstraction that an object becomes more real than the real; what a revolutionary discovery it was, when Paul Cézanne suddenly realized that he no longer painted landscapes but literally pictures, not mountains and houses but triangles and rectangles, not content but form. Yet there is an inherent conflict between the attempts to elevate art and the desire to be grounded in reality, between the aesthetic truths of the point, line and plane on the one hand, and the persuasive power of representation on the other. Nothing is more powerful than the power of the example.

* * *

With these comments on abstraction and rhetoric constantly in mind, I now return to the picture of the American football. I cannot really explicate how and why, but when I look at this peculiar image with my eyes closed, then I see that the shell of the oval consists of a set of tightly packed threads, sometimes shaped as a double helix sometimes as a Moebius band. Graphically:

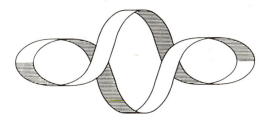

From the center of this figure rules the dematerialized point, the origo of imagination. Along the innumerable threads which connect the eight fix-points of silence lie the transition forms of human conduct, always in flux yet always kept in place by its dialectical counterparts of individual and society. These forces of checks and balances can themselves be represented by a set of lines, all running through the dematerialized point at an angle. I have set this angle equal to 45 degrees, partly because Kandinsky insisted that the diagonal is the most talkative of lines, mainly because I thereby introduce assymetry (hence movement) into the otherwise symmetrical figures. Whether the resulting drawings remind me more of the biological scriptures of the DNA or of the alternating currents in an electric generator I do not know. At any rate, the dialectical forces can be depicted as follows[1]:

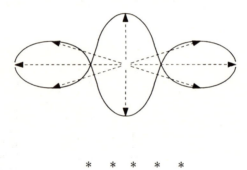

* * * * *

As illustrations and elaborations, I now proceed to a brief presentation of two sets of cases. The first approaches the speech of silence and thereby some crucial forms of socialization: By which means are we made so obedient and so predictable? The second captures the silence of speech and thereby some well known modes of understanding: Through which categories do I learn about difference and by which languages do we establish the same?

1 It should be reemphasized that the lines of the dialectical forces run through the dematerialized point at angles of 45 degrees. The discrepancy between the text and the drawing is therefore not real but apparent, an unavoidable result of projecting a three-dimensional image onto a two-dimensional plane. Yet I shall be the first to testify that lodged inside a rotating football it is easy to get dizzy.

In my imagination, the double helix of socialization is drawn as

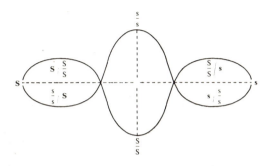

while that of understanding looks like

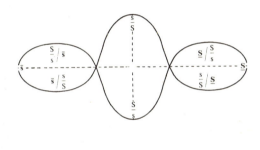

*

What now remains to discover is a set of empirical examples which can be attached to the noted transition forms. In a sense, the two schemes as hitherto presented are mute, for they are *langue* without *parole*. To get them to speak, I must therefore link the generic names of the drawings with a set of illustrative cases, not unlike what Bertrand Russell did with his theory of proper names and definite descriptions, and not unlike what Carl von Linné did in his *Flora Suecica*. The difficulties are nevertheless tremendous, for in the realm of thought-and-action the meaning of a name is not given by the object it denotes but by the context in which it occurs.

Here almost everything is hidden. What I shall pass over in the space of a sentence, others have covered in yards of books. Yet I cannot resist the temptation. Can't stop me now! Out it comes, a small but representative cut from the imagined *Flora* of thought-and-action. First some specimens collected in the deep forests of socialization. Then some colorful growths from the open fields of understanding.

*

S   s

the *REPRESSED*, desire of the completely obedient.

the *SUBLIME*, without a trace swept under the threshold.

$$S / \frac{S}{S} \qquad s / \frac{s}{s}$$

the transition form of the *fetish*, a material object of magical powers. Arrest of the metonymic, expression of the belief that lifeless things have a spirit, that a stone is more than a stone, a bear tooth more than a bear tooth, a shoe more than a shoe. And yet one should never ignore the power of Bertrand Russell's remark that "a robust sense of reality is very necessary in framing a correct analysis of propositions about unicorns, golden mountains, round squares and other pseudo-objects". The practice of operationalization belongs to the ideology of materialism and

the transition form of the *icon*, an attempt to picture the non-picturable. Liberation of the metaphoric. A holy image, a link between God and Man, a symbol of incarnation. The light of an icon comes from everywhere, for it is not the viewer who looks at an image but the image that looks at a viewer. Perspective is reversed, time cancelled out. The icon has no frame, yet it lies at the heart of western culture. The Iconoclastic Controversy is itself a consequence of Christianity's double roots, one in Judaism with its prohibition against graven images, the other in Hellenism with speaks the rhetoric of the concrete. I know for a fact what a fact is. *Factum-verum*. Man the forger forging the uncreated conscience of his race. Phallus of the phallus.

$$\frac{S}{S}$$

silence of *STONES*, word without meaning. Petrified matter.

$$\frac{S}{S}/s$$

the transition form of the holy *communion*, the ritual sharing of beliefs. Performance of ontological transformations in which wine turns to blood turns to love. Incarnation in reverse. Submission under the social pressures of being normal, of not being alone with the nonexpressable. The refusniks are in deed frightening: the hermit, the autist, the anorectic. How do I know difference and how do we share the same? *Corpus domini nostri Jesu Christi custodiat animam tuam in vitam aeternam*

s

CONVERTED. Eternal life. Ether of Mount Olympus.

its habit of representing the gods in statues. *Homo erectus*. Trust as a matter of obedience. Belief as rememberance of members dismembered.

$$\frac{s}{s}$$

silence of *SPIRITS*, meaning without words. Evaporating mind.

$$\frac{s}{s}/S$$

the transition form of the state *prison*, legalized means of correction. Discipline and punish, institutionalization of the idea that the body is the mind's corrective. Operationalization as thingification, the power of the eye and the index finger. Yet there is an unthinkable difference between a body in chains and a mind without desire, between classes of objects and unique individuals. *Cogito ergo sum* yields first to *Desidero ergo sum*, then to *Desiderare ergo sum*. Therefore I sentence you to

S

CONVICTED. Monstrous death. Rocks of Scylla and Carybdis.

Graphically:

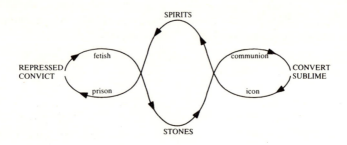

*

| s̄ | s̲ |

| the *sublime*, recreation of the invisible, uncovering the marvellous. | the *repressed*. Violence of the social. Hiding the scar of the horrible. |

$\bar{s} / \frac{s}{S}$ $\underline{s} / \frac{S}{s}$

the transition form of *inwardness*, the mode of understanding which is in the poetry of Søren Kierkegaard and Stéphane Mallarmé. The fact that existence is unspeakable does not mean that it is nothing, for what cannot be said can sometimes be shown. Within the prisonhouse of language, every thought gives off a throw of dice, not a predetermined verdict but perhaps a constellation. There is an echo in Mallarmé's cry for his dead son: "It is you that I want, you and in

the transition form of *outwardness*, the mode of understanding which is in the science of Karl Marx and the politics of the twentieth century. It is not enough to understand the world, the point is to change it. Yet, not even Marx himself was a pure materialist, for it was he who stated that "even though relations between commodities initially may appear as relations between things, they are in fact relations between people". What distinguishes the worst of architects you myself". Man is not a stone but a living being with the courage of giving an answer that is not an answer. "Predicament" is the name of the game, "anxiety" the price of the unnameable. All that is solid melts into air.

from the best of bees is that the former raises his structure in the mind before he builds it in wax. And yet, "paradox" is the analyst's major enemy, "tragedy" the inevitable outcome. All that is vapourish soldifies into matter.

$$\frac{s}{S}$$

the silence of *religion*, the art of I and Thou.

$$\frac{S}{s}$$

the silence of *politics*, the practice of delegation.

$$\frac{s}{S} / \underline{S}$$

The transition form of the *symbolic*. Fly in the ceiling of Solomon's Temple, Chagall's blue bride over mythical rooftops, bull's eye.

$$\frac{S}{s} / \bar{S}$$

the transition form of the *real*. Malevich's white square on white, plane of the taken-for-granted, Mose's tablets.

$$\underline{S} \qquad \bar{s}$$

the repressed of the double. Killing of Girard's *scapegoat*. Scream in the desert. Death of an individual. Birth of the social.

the sublime of Veronica's *kerchief*, twist of an eye, tone of a voice. Birth of an individual, death of the social.

Graphically:

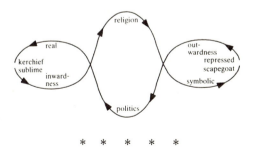

* * * * *

49

Mystical figures, creatures of imagination. Cure and poison in the same breath. Memory of Pharmakon, dream of dreams. Seeing that the naked eye is blind.

The *Anemona Nemorosa* of the Linnean system is characterized by its own sexuality. Although I tried, I could never figure it out. What I do know, however, is that the same flower weaves the white carpet over which fairies dance in spring-time. And in my own country school every ten-year old was certain that *Prostafis Luctarilla* comes with a special flagrance and a bombastic bang.

A promise is a promise. But in the drunkenness of the Bar de Saussure I have been told that desire cannot be named. Yet I know how to recall them: Anna, Mona, Emma, Rosa. All in my herbarium.

* * * * *

Claude Mellan FORMATUR UNICUS UNA non alter, *THE ONE FORMING THE ONE no other*

Auerbach E, 1953 (German original, 1946) *Mimesis: The Representation of Reality in Western Literature* (Princeton University Press, Princeton)

Brown N O, 1974 *Closing Time* (Vintage, New York)

Cassirer E, 1953-57 (German originals, 1923-29) *The Philosophy of Symbolic Forms* (Yale University Press, New Haven)

Derrida J, 1987 (French original, 1978) *The Truth in Painting* (University of Cicago Press, Chicago)

Focillon H, 1989 (French original, 1934) *The Life of Forms in Art* (Zone Books, New York)

Freud S, 1950 (German original, 1913) *Totem and Taboo* (Routledge & Kegan Paul, London)

Girard R, 1987 (French original, 1978) *Things Hidden Since the Foundation of the World* (Stanford University Press, Stanford)

Hegel G W F, 1977 (German original, 1807) *Phenomenology of Spirit* (Clarendon Press, Oxford)

Joyce J, 1934 (Original, 1922) *Ulysses* (New Library, New York)

Joyce J, 1958 (Original, 1939) *Finnegans Wake* (Viking, New York)

Kandinsky W, 1977 (German original, 1914) *Concerning the Spiritual in Art* (Dover, New York)

Kandinsky W, 1979 (German original, 1926) *Point and Line to Plane* (Dover, New York)

Kant I, 1966 (German original, 1781) *Critique of Pure Reason* Doubleday, Garden City, NY)

Kant I, 1949 (German original, 1788) *Critique of Practical Reason* (University of Chicago Press, Chicago)

Kant I, 1951 (German original, 1790) *Critique of Judgment* (Harper, New York)

Kierkegaard S, 1959 (Danish original, 1843) *Either/Or* (Princeton University Press, Princeton)

Kristeva J, 1987 (French original, 1983) *Tales of Love* (Columbia University Press, New York)

Lacan J, 1977 (French original, 1966) *Écrits: A Selection* (Tavistock, London)

Lachterman D R, 1989 *The Ethics of Geometry: A Genealogy of Modernity* (Routledge, New York)

Lacoue-Labarthe P, 1989 (French originals, 1975-86) *Typography: Mimesis, Philosophy, Politics* (Harvard University Press, Cambridge MA)

Malevich K, 1968 (Russian originals, 1915-33) *Essays on Art* (Borgen, Copenhagen)

Mallarmé S, 1977 (French original of "Un coup de dés", 1897) *The Poems* (Penguin, Harmondsworth)

Mallarmé S, 1983 (French original, 1961, written in the 1870's) *A Tomb for Anatole* (North Point Press, San Francisco)

Marx K, 1967 (German original, 1867-94) *Capital* (International Publishers, New York)

Merleau-Ponty M, 1968 (French original, 1964) *The Visible and the Invisible* (Northwestern University Press, Evanston)

Musil R, 1979 (German original, 1930-4) *The Man Without Qualities* (Picador, London)

Nietzsche F, 1968 (German originals 1883-88) *The Will to Power* (Vintage, New York)

Olsson G, 1980 *Birds in Egg/Eggs in Bird* (Pion, London)

Olsson G, 1990 *Antipasti* (Korpen, Göteborg)

Olsson G, 1991 *Lines of Power/Limits of Language* (University of Minnesota

Press, Minneapolis)
Olsson G, 1991 "Malevic sfigurato" *Slam* 3
Olsson G, 1991 "Invisible Maps: A Prospectus" *Geografiska Annaler* 73 B 85-91
Panofsky E, 1991 (German original, 1927) *Perspective as Symbolic Form* (Zone Books, New York)
de Saussure F, 1983 (French notes, 1907-11) *Course in General Linguistics* (Duckworth, London)
Spencer Brown G, 1969 *Laws of Form* (George Allen & Unwin, London)
Stella F, 1986 *Working Space* (Harvard University Press, Cambridge MA)
Vernant J-P, Vidal-Naquet P, 1990 (French originals, 1972-86) *Myth and Tragedy in Ancient Greece* (Zone Books, New York)
Watson J D, 1968 *The Double Helix* (Atheneum, New York)
Whitehead A N, Russell B, 1910-13 *Principia Mathematica* (Cambridge University Press, Cambridge)
Wittgenstein L, 1961 (Bilingual original, 1922) *Tractatus Logico-Philosophicus* (Routledge & Kegan Paul, London)
Wittgenstein L, 1953 *Philosophische Untersuchungen / Philosophical Investigations* (Basil Blackwell, Oxford)

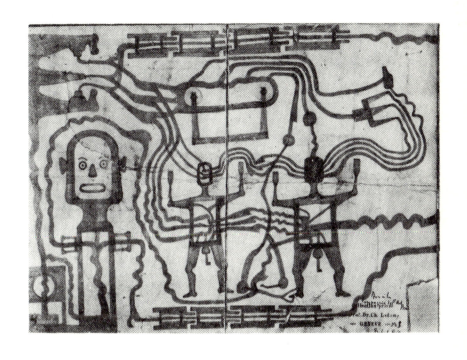

Robert Gie: Systeme cosmique de circulation d'efluves

RED RIVER VALLEY:
GEO-GRAPHICAL STUDIES IN THE LANDSCAPE OF LANGUAGE

by Ole Michael Jensen

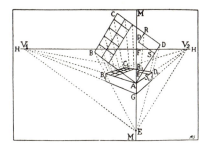 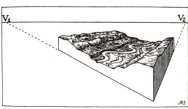

Four lines
Two peripheral and visible
two central and invisible
That's the whole scheme

Morphology of the landscape

Limits of language are limits of silence, limits of representation are limits of speech. Through the landscape of language runs a stream of representation. On one side of the valley is the waving curtain of pure spirituality. On the other the hard wall of pure physicality. Behind the mountain ranges, and marked by the limits of language, lie on one side the realm of the silence of silence, on the other that of the silence of noise. The silence behind the curtain is white. The silence behind the wall is black. Traces of traces as opposed to frozen energy, the blank page as opposed to signature all over. Mind and matter ready to intermingle on the scene of writing.

The limits of language are two. One marks the silence of signs without meaning, the other the silence of meaning without signs.

Just as artists find themselves matted in the curtain of whiteness, politicians knock their heads against the wall of blackness. Climbing the white mountains is a quest for expression. Climbing the black mountains is a quest for meaning.

The river of representation cleaves the realm of language into two, not unlike what took place at the beginning of creation, when God made heaven and earth, day and night, white and black. A cut and a name, a spark from a Michelangelan index finger.

On one of the river banks stands Saussure with his sign

$$\frac{s}{S}$$

on the other Lacan with his

$$\frac{S}{s}$$

Although both would like to reach down to the bottom of the river, to the holy Line of Power, they must be satisfied with merely naming only its limits; the signs are the nameable limits of the invisible bottom. The water itself not only separates the shores but also touches them, calmly and self-referentially. In the acts of understanding and overcoming thought and sensitivity are fused together in a stream of perfect representation.

Two realms of language, each delimited by a river on the one side and a mountain range on the other. One of the language realms lies between the Saussurean sign of speech (s/S) and the curtain of whiteness (s/s), the other between the Lacanian sign of speech (S/s) and the wall of blackness (S/S). The river itself constitutes yet another form of silence. This is red, because it is the silence of language (Kandinsky, 1979).

	THE SILENCE OF NOISE	
	(The black mountains of matter)	
The wall of blackness		$\frac{S}{S}$
	The plain of black speech	
--		$\frac{S}{S}$
	THE SILENCE OF LANGUAGE (The red river of perfect representation)	$\frac{S}{S}$
--		
	The plain of white speech	
The curtain of whiteness		$\frac{S}{S}$
	THE SILENCE OF SILENCE	
	(The white mountains of mind)	

Figure 1: A map showing the morphology of the landscape of language.

Topography of the landscape

In the terminology of Charles Sander Peirce, the landscape of language can be related to the three fields of *pure grammar*, *logic proper* and *pure rhetoric*. Each of these fields is covered by three kinds of signs, termed *icons*, *indices* and *symbols* respectively. An icon refers to the denoted object merely by virtue of similarity, even though the object may have no material existence. An index refers to the denoted object by virtue of being really affected by the object. A symbol refers to the denoted object by virtue of a social code, possibly embedded in an imaginary universe to which the symbol refers (Peirce, 1955, pp.98-119). Put differently, a symbol expresses a relation with an index and an icon, an index a relation with an icon, and an icon a relation with itself.

Peirce's semiotics, as his entire philosophy, is triadic. This implies that his term "firstness" always refers to what exists per se, "secondness" to what exists only by or in reaction to something prior, "thirdness" to what mediates between firstness and secondness. Thus icon is firstness, index secondness and symbol thirdness. Taken together, these signs nevertheless belong to the secondness level of Peirce's trichotomy, i.e. to that level which is concerned with the relation of the sign to its object.[1]

Signs belong strictly to the landscape of language, themselves shaping its surface. Since sign is secondness, so is language, a reaction to something prior, which might be meaningful (Bateson, 1987). And yet, every text is embedded in an invisible context of thirdness. It is with the secondness, i.e. with the "de-sign" of this thirdness (mythology), that the present study is concerned. Put differently, the landscape of language contains a metaphysical meta-interpretant. A study of that is left for the professor.

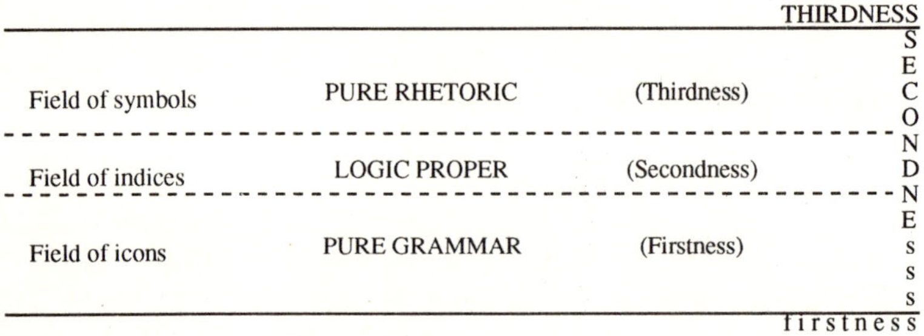

		THIRDNESS
Field of symbols	PURE RHETORIC	(Thirdness)
Field of indices	LOGIC PROPER	(Secondness)
Field of icons	PURE GRAMMAR	(Firstness)

S E C O N D N E S S

firstness

Figure 2: A map showing the topography of the landscape of Language

Settling the landscape

In the realm of language, there are only differences. "Whether we take the signified or the signifier, language has neither ideas nor sounds that existed before the linguistic system, but only conceptual and phonic differences that have issued from the system".(Saussure, 1959, p. 120). Hence only reflections and reminiscences can float along in the river of representation. After crawling through a swamp of differences, these species of the trace eventually reach one of the dry areas of speech. By participating in the exchange of signs – through the transformation and interchange between representation

---

1 *The first trichotomy refers to the quality of "the sign in itself", the second to the relation of "the sign to the object", the third to the character of "the sign as an interpretant" (Peirce, 1955, p.101).*

and narrative[2] – they become themselves representable, i.e. indexed into a social order and thereby made present. By climbing onto the shore, the species changes into a *homo significator*.

Semiotic man leads a twofold existence in the landscape of language: as an original man and as a subspecies. The original man can *live* only on the right bank adjacent to the curtain of whiteness. The subspecies then crosses the river of representation to settle down and to *be-li(e)ve* on the left bank adjacent to the wall of blackness. On the right bank, in the field of pure grammar, the original and *anthropo-logical* man is at home. On the left bank, in the field of pure rhetoric, dwells *grapho-logical* man.

In the terminology of Ferdinand Tönnies, the right bank is the world of "Gemeinschaft", the left, although built upon the grammar of the former, is that of "Gesellschaft" (Tönnies, 1963). In the world of Gemeinschaft, map and territory are the same, present and represented cannot be split apart. The third field of Peirce's semiotics, pure rhetoric, does not yet exist. By contrast, navigators in the world of Gesellschaft may realize that "the map is not the territory" (Korzybski, 1941). The present and the represented are separated, once and for all; orienteering in the two worlds is vastly different.[3] In crossing the river between the two worlds, graphological man tastes the silent power of The Equal-Sign. Moving into the new territory he does not, as yet, notice the limits of representation.

For settlers on the bank of Gemeinschaft, reference to personal experience is taboo. A body that moves around on the right bank has no existence if it does not fit into the pure grammar, the blueprint of anthropologos, the taken-for-granted in a discourse without a subject, in short *doxa* (Bourdieu, 1977).[4] Thus the accumulated personal experience can only be redeemed in the *community* by a ritual

---

2 *An expression impresses itself as a trace on a body. A narrative expresses itself as a body of traces (a representation). Put differently, a representation can be perceived only as a narrative.*

3 *Kant, the first clairvoyant of the new world, makes a distinction between "das Ding als Erscheinung" and "das Ding an sich". Heidegger's work also deals with this, and more important still: he did realize that Gesellschaft cannot exist separated from Gemeinschaft.*

4 *It is this taken-for-granted that structuralists call structure.*

killing followed by ritual rebirth, i.e. a trans-lation of the body (as an icon) from one social category (an index) to another, supervised by the community (van Gennep, 1960). This is the way a person remains (a symbol) in re-lation with community, the way he remains on the *plain of doxa* (Jensen, 1991).

Expanding the territory on the Gesellschaft bank is an individual appearance in itself. Still, experiences are tabooed, but this time traces of "footprints" have to correlate with the Map, to what has so far been accepted as a consistent representation of the *society*, in short *orthodoxy*. To be accepted, the solipsistic letter in mind has to be printed out in the presence of a community, i.e. coined in language by language. Even true belief of Descartes has to undergo a ritual of graphological baptizing witnessed by the "guards of orthodoxy".[5]

Just like the priests of Gemeinschaft function as travel agents preparing the travelers for trans-lation, psychoanalysts who take part in the life of Gesellschaft function as doctors restoring the re-lation to the Gemeinschaft, especially for those who have lost their way in the new territory.

The two worlds belong to drastically different epistemes even though Gesellschaft cannot exist without Gemeinschaft. Gemeinschaft and Gesellschaft have their individual cultures, each tilling their own part of the river valley. Gemeinschaft (iconic culture) does not and cannot pay any attention to the notation "culture", indeed to the "notation culture", whereas Gesellschaft (symbolic culture) would not be Gesellschaft without it. The former is the cult of cultivating land, the latter the cult of cultivating culture.

The offspring of anthropological man undertakes an odyssey beyond the fence of the horizon which man has had since the beginning of the world. When anthropological man leaves the plain of doxa, crossing The Line of Power, he actually interferes with the

---

5 *Since we are in fact imitating (the ideal of) God's baptizing, it has been necessary to invent the Popperian principle of falsification.*

deity. In so doing he is split into mind and body, an icon guided by an interpretant, thus creating symbols.

As the descendant of classical man, modern man has to trust what he thus far has believed: God's monopolistic use of representation. By crossing the Line, he threatens God's privilege, and without knowing it finds himself engaged in the project of enlightenment. In the de-fencing of his new territory, he keeps strangers out by engraving orthodoxies into something solid, the doxa of Gemeinschaft. Transferred onto the map of morphology, the left river bank rose to the surface as *the ex-plains of orthodoxy*. It eventually became impossible to kill the bodies of all enemies, a change which marks the transition from classical to modern modes of life. Killing words instead of bodies, symbols instead of icons, gradually became the predominant praxis of warfare.

The domain of graphological man	GESELLSCHAFT be-li(e)ving	The left river bank: the ex-plains of orthodoxy
	The swamp of differences	
The domain of anthropological man	GEMEINSCHAFT living	The right river bank: the plain of doxa

Figure 3: A map showing the anthropology of the landscape of language

The genesis of the landscape

In birth, graphological man cuts his own navel string. René Girard (1987) has traced this string back to the expulsion of the very first scapegoat, to the very first social difference, to the foundation of the world. A tribe member was arbitrarily singled out, expelled and killed as the instigator of escalating violence. This scapegoating actually unified – and purified – the tribe as a whole. But it also marked the difference between the tribe and the One and Only. This was the original Michelangelan cut, immediately transferred to the absent (the silence of language). This Absent was then sacralized as the founder of peace; a cut in the name of God, the birth of Deity, but also the mark of transition from 'biologos' to 'anthropologos'.

The genesis of the landscape has its origo. This point is located in that spot of the battlefield, where the pupil of the collective eye meets that of the One and Only. This is the spot, where the aim of the mimetic desire converges on one particular victim. A member of the tribe becomes a scapegoat, to be killed and soon after sacralized. And out of the ground of the holy point of that first sacrifice wells a spring, the spring of the Red River. The marks on the bottom of that river are the traces left by the original scapegoat. The power of the tribe members, absorbed by desire of desire, converges into one moving point which in turn constitutes the invisible Line of Power. Fertilized by the sacred water of the Red River, the right river bank is itself sacralized and baptized.

To summarize:
• The genesis of the Genesis of the landscape of language (The Origo) is the place of the first collective agreement on some-body's guilt.
• Power (The Line of Power) generates from the scapegoat mechanism manifested by a collective murder.
• Signification (The Equal Sign) generates from the process of sacrificing.
• The initial settlement occurs on the fertile shores of the sacred land. Later, there is a migration across the river, where new land is occupied. The former territory lies on the right bank and is the plain of doxa, that of Gemeinschaft. The latter lies on the left bank and is formed by the ex-plains orthodoxy, that of Gesellschaft.

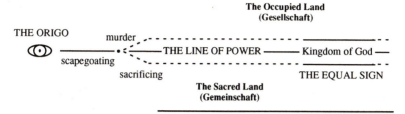

Figure 4: The genesis of the landscape of Language

Jacques Derrida is the expert in river crossings. His philosophy of différance deals with swimming in the river of representation, but also with the interpretation of the footprints left on the banks. The subject constitutes it-self by 'spacing (and) tracing'. In the river stream, solipsistic writing by erasing (archi-writing). On the bank of common ground, social expression by deferral. Inside and outside the stream. Imprint and expression, but always on the "scene of writing" (Derrida, 1978).

Homo Grammaticus is, for Derrida, the name of the species. When Homo Grammaticus climbs out of the Red River of death, the footprints he leaves are themselves traces of difference deferred, always already present in what was before and in what follows after.

A point set in motion
split into two
Difference deferred
That's the point.

References

Asplund J, 1991 *Essä om Gemeinschaft och Gesellschaft* (Korpen, Stockholm)

Bateson G, 1987, (First published 1972) "The Science of Mind and Order" in *Steps to an Ecology of Mind* (Jason Aronson Inc., London)

Bourdieu P, 1977 (French original, 1972), *Outline of a Theory of Praxis* (Cambridge University Press, Cambridge)

Carse J P, 1987 (First published 1966) *Finite and Infinite Games* (Penguin Books, Hammonworth)

Derrida J, 1978 (French original, 1967) *Writing and Difference*. (The University of Chicago Press, Chicago)

Derrida J, 1979 (French/English version) *Spurs/Ésperon, Nietzsches Styles/Les Styles de Nietzsche* (The University of Chicago Press, Chicago)

Derrida J, 1982 (French original 1972), "Différance" in *Margins of Philosophy* (The Harvester Press, Brighton)

Foucault M, 1979 (French original, 1975) *Discipline and Punish: the Birth of the Prison* (Penguin, Harmonworth)

van Gennep A, 1960 (French original, 1908) *The Rites of Passage*. (The University of Chicago, Chicago)

Girard R, 1987 (French original, 1978) *Things Hidden Since the Foundation of the World* (The Athlone Press, London)

Girard R, 1977 (French original, 1972) *Violence and the Sacred* (The Johns Hopkins University Press, Baltimore)

Jensen O.M., 1991 *Herrens Tabernakel* (Nordplans Meddelande 1991:1, Stockholm). An English version: Lords Tabernacle, in manuscript.

Kandinsky W, 1979 (German original, 1926) *Point and Line to Plane* (Dover Publications, New York)

Korzybski A, 1941 *Science and Sanity* (Science Press, New York)

Lacan J, 1977 (French original, 1966, *Écrits: A Selection* (Tavistock, London)

Mauss M, 1925 (French original, 1925) *The Gift* (Norton, New York)

Olsson G, 1987, "The Social Space of Silence" *Environment and Planning D: Society and Space* **5** 249-262

Olsson G, 1991a, "Invisible Maps: A Prospectus" *Geografiska Annaler*. 73B 85-92

Olsson G, 1991b *Lines of Power/ Limits of Language* (University of Minnesota Press, Minneapolis)

Peirce C S, 1955 (Originals 1867-1906) *Philosophical Writings of Peirce* Ed. J. Buchler (Dover Publications, New York)

de Saussure F, 1966 (French notes, 1907-11) *Course in General Linguistics* (McGrow-Hill, New York).

Tönnies F, 1963 (German original, 1887) *Community and Society* (Harper and Row, New York)

RITES OF TRESPASSING

A play by Ole Michael Jensen and Dagmar Reichert

Stage with 3 zones (2 gates each), confession chair in the middle zone, audience in the third zone.
White paint, black paint, brushes, map, handkerchief, white sheet, black sheet, veil, bucket.

Characters:
A woman (W)
A (male) priest (P)

The poem on p.XXXX is translated after Hildegard v. Bingen 1141 (In: Hildegard v. Bingen, 1990: Gott sehen, Piper München)

First performance: Bagni di Lucca, June 1991

* * *

Lights on.
Woman and priest are in the middle zone, he sitting higher in the confession chair, she kneeling at his side.

W: Yes father.

P: I understand. So you need some help. But you must know that it is not me, who would help you. Only God can do that.

W: But I was told by my grandmother that I should come to see you! She said that you would be the one who could help me. And she has been telling me stories about all those you have helped before.

P: God has helped them. I only assisted them in finding God's way and the Holy Gate to begin their journey.
... Tell me more...

W: I do not want to be a woman.

P: No?

W: No! I do not want to become like my mother. I do not want to stay at home with a bunch of kids and wait for my husband to return from work and then to fall asleep in front of the television.

P: Well, your description is a bit... Do you not think your mother knows very well what she is doing?

W: I do not want to do that! ... On the other hand: There are these men. – But they have such strange expectations about women! I am not "this calm enchanting being, the mysterious ship gliding over the dark sea promising happiness and retirement..." It is the truth! They talk like that!

P: Yes, girl, but only at the beginning!

W: I do not like the beginning and I do not like the end!

P: So what would you like?

W: I would like to be able to be myself. In work for example: Where I work now there are almost only men. They continuously want to give me their advice: What I should do, what is important for me to read, how I should write... They think that I cannot take the responsibility for myself. And then I always have to fight – and be very tough and very arrogant and good in pretending that everything is under control – at least as good as they are.

P: Well, if you manage it...

W: Yes, but I do not want to do that. I do not want to be like them.

P: I see.

W: There is something else.

P: Yes?

W: You know this "bonds of love" story: I mean ..., you know, this domination and submission and one must be the strong and one must be the weak, and clear positions, above and below, and... I do not function this way. It is more... (*mixing gesture*). You know?

P: I can imagine... So, in sum: you do not want to be a proper woman, or – at least – you do not want to be what you think the others consider proper for a woman. Hmmm... There is ... There is in our society also a place for someone like you!

W: So you mean you could help me? I would ... I could be myself and still be acceptable to my parents and my colleagues and my friends? You think there is a place for someone like me?

P: Yes! Naturally!

W: But why did I not... I really have been looking for it... I... I cannot imagine such a place!

P: Well, maybe I have a bit more experience... (*laughing indulgently*) Do you not want to leave a little bit for me to do as well? – I think I can help you. Do you want me to?

W: Yes!

P: So I will. I will make you up for a journey. While your body will travel, your mind will change all by itself. (*Stands up*) Come over here!

W: (*Stands up, hesitating*) I think I am a little afraid.

P: You do not need to be afraid. Just close your eyes and relax. Believe me: God knows how to trans-late your mind by trans-ferring your body. And by his will, I will do what needs to be done. (*Starts* *painting her face white, covering her with a veil*) Slowly you will forget the old values, the image of "woman" that you have had troubles with. It can touch you no longer, your body becomes unreachable for the others, and gradually you yourself will forget who you are. Never mind, nobody... (*leads her to the gate*)

W: Never mind? My eyes... I cannot see clearly anymore. Where are you leading me? I feel a threshold. Is it an exit? An entrance? I am afraid!

P: (*To her*) You do not have to shake. Trust me! I am a priest. (*To audience*): Her body is dis-appearing, she is becoming invisible. This is what has to happen – since the beginning of time. She did not have the proper consciousness any more, she questioned the fundamental differences of God's order. Very dangerous! Very dangerous! Her desire could have destroyed the whole. People change, we cannot do anything about it, but we must take care that they change in an orderly way. Precisely. If she does not like her traditional female role, she must turn into somebody else: A Feminist. This should do.

(*To her, still leading her*) Trust me. I am putting you on the right track. I only want the best for you and all of us.

W: (*Slowly bending down, near the edge of the gate*) Something is going on inside me, beating in my throat, I do not know... I think ... I think... my thoughts are drowning, dissolving... I feel... sliding, sinking inside... I hear it... my blood?... louder and louder...

P: (*To the audience*) She is crossing the boundary to The Beyond. She is afraid and confused, as everybody I have seen on this threshold before. They do not know that they are led by the invisible hand of the Lord, led by The Father, The Son and The Holy Spirit, guided by an Angel directly into the Lord's Tabernacle.

W: Oh magnificent colour,
rooted in the sun,
shining in luminous brightness
in a circle
human mind cannot grasp:

You are surrounded
by embraces of Godly secrets.
You are glittering like the dawn.
You glow in the flames of the sun. (*She disappears*)

P: (*To the audience*) Now she is on her way, somewhere out there with the wild women. They are witches, they fly through the air and dance in a circle, faster and faster, singing with the howling wind. You would best never hear them! Beautiful voices, enchanting and irresistable. But you would be drawn near them and they would charm you with sweet song and you would join them in the flower-strewn fields where they lie, while around them the bodies of their victims lie in heaps. – I myself need not to be afraid of them, because I am a man of God, bound to the law of the father. But those who are not prepared by a priest will never return home. I have prepared her. But this was only the first part of my duty. Now I have to pray to God and ask him to give me the strength to bring her back when she has finished The Passage. Then I have to baptize her back into this world. (*Praying*) You (*Pointing to the audience*) shall be my witnesses. (*Goes away*)

(*Comes back with black paint*) God is merciful with this girl. (*Points to paint/brush*) He gave me the distinctive power I need. Soon she will return to our world. She will come up right here. Here the womb of the world will open up, here I will stand and wait for her. (*Waits*)

W: (*After some time she comes up, but through another gate. She remains ON the boundary (half/half). She is all wet, the white color in her face is half washed off, the veil torn. She first spits out a mouthful of water and cleans her eyes*)
Fading out? Is it fading away? Becoming heavy, does it not flow anymore? I see... things taking shape. Why does it not continue as it was? What was it? It was so... so... full of light. Why did it spit me out? I think... I think there is a difference... What happened? Is it really over? (*Touches realm inside boundary*) Over here?

P: (*Notices her. To himself, nervous*) She is there! Why is she there? Something must have gone wrong, Oh God! I have done something wrong! Now she may be a monster (*looks, but cannot recognize enough*), half fish, half woman maybe, not fully born! I must go and deliver her! (*To her*) Here, poor creature, wretched daughter of Lilith, give me your hands, (*loud*) I will pull you out! (*Pulls her arm*)

W: Hey, psst! I have a headache. Why do you make such a noise?

P: I have to save you! I will pull on your neck... (*does that*)

W: (*Pushes him away. To herself*) Idiot! Little understanding of women this man has! This gruesome earnestness and clumsy importunity with which he tries to grasp me! I think I remember them. These men. Yes, it was long time ago, something has happened, but I remember. And I remember me. That *me*. But now it is all different, all dissolved... Still, I must not forget.

P: (*Tries to pull again*) You have to do a little bit yourself too, you are not so light! Why do you hesitate, trust me, I will guide you into the new world.

W: Are you a travel agent?

P: Yes... No. But I also can point out to you a nice place and a good time, a history you will appreciate. Everything is prepared for you. Once you are over here, I can entitle you: You will be a "Feminist". Give me your hands now, do not stay there, it is too dangerous!

W: (*Stretching*) Why is it so dangerous? It feels very nice, I enjoy it! Why do you want me to *be* something? ... I do not care very much about these titles. What was it... did you say "Feminist"?

P: Yes! You have to be baptized "Feminist"! The witnesses are waiting. (*Points out at the audience*) There!

W: Baptized a Feminist? I have no idea what that could *be*, a Feminist!

P: (*To the audience*) I think it did go well after all: She has forgotten everything. But now I have to introduce her to the new order. (*To her*) Maybe you are a little tired, you look a bit disordered, but you do not have to worry. I will take care of you.

W: What do you *mean* by "a Feminist"?

P: Slowly, slowly! I will explain everything to you: A Feminist is someone who supports Feminism.

W: Hmmm.. and Feminism?

P: Feminism is a position in our society. A political position, maybe cultural too. It is the position of the Feminists.

W: Of all of them?

P: By definition. It is quite easy, everybody knows who they are – they all look a bit the same – and everybody knows, more or less, what they want.

W: What *do* they want?

P: They want a better position for women in society.

W: Sounds like a good idea.

P: You see! That is why I am offering you this name! We need women who fight against patriarchy. They need to bring us back into closer contact with nature! And we need women who demonstrate the importance of not being objective, not being analytic, not concentrating on the mind. We need someone who tries to introduce a language that is not the traditional male one. There is a lot to be done! Up to now, for example, not even *female* scientists have given the question of language a prominent position on their agenda!

W: ... If this is what Feminism is, it is nothing for me. I do not want to do anything like that!

P: But why!? You cannot stay where you are, have you forgotten...

W: No, I have not. That is why I do not want to be the other, the negative. Negativity at the most, I still feel it, the strength, the rhythm, the flow... I am far too fluid to be negative!

P: But it is not negative! Feminism is very positive! It is a solid political position, a serious one!

W: Yes, I know, but I cannot be anything that is solid. I am not the right person for it.

P: Now wait! What do you mean by "not the right person"!? Where you are now you are not a person at all, you are nobody! You are nowhere and nobody, nothing, not even a mer(e)maid it seems. You are *invisible*!

W: I do not care.

P: But you have to be somebody! What if someone asks you for your ID?

W: I thought you said I am invisible...

P: *You* thought! Who is this "you"? Your words do not mean anything!

W: And who are *you* talking to? I do not have to ask what I already know. That you are not nobody, for example. Who are you anyway?

P: This is stupid! (*Formal*) Please come out now.

W: Who the hell are you!?

P: (*Determined*) I am a priest!

W: Oh, excuse me.

P: (*Determined*) I am the priest and it is my holy duty to baptize you. It is time to finish this useless discussion. Come out, and let me give you this mark. (*Tries to mark her forehead with black paint*) It does not hurt. Afterwards we can all have a big feast. Good food and Italian wine. This is the tradition!

W: I have nothing against tradition, but it is your tradition, not mine. Thank you for the invitation, but I feel very comfortable and happy as I am. – There is something I would like to think through. I need a little time for myself now.

P: For yourself, who ever that is...

W: Listen, I have absolutely no intention of doing something now, even if it is going to your Feminist feast.

P: My Feminist feast!

W: I do not want to hurt you, old father, but, you know what, leave me alone.

P: What an individualistic hedonist you are! It is very important to fight for the Feminist issues! All women should be Feminists! Yes, I am a man, but I will show you that even I am willing do something: You are a woman, but if you come over here now, I will guarantee

you a job almost as powerful as that of a priest.
W: What does a priest have to do?
P: Hmm...
W: This, there in your pocket. What is it?
P: It is a map. I am a geographer.
W: Oh, you are not just a priest, but a geographer too?
P: Well, it is a bit the same.
W: So what does a priest-geographer have to do?
P: Hmm...
W: Tell me...
P: Well: They have to know the way. They have to guide bodies from one world into another.
W: Really?? But do *other* people want to leave their world?
P: Not "want to", maybe, but have to, when their time has come.
W: When their time has come?
P: Yes. When stability demands change. When the continuity of society demands that certain individuals take a new position. Then God, the protector of the social order sends them to me.
W: (*To herself*) So they are not like me. They are ones that are *sent* to him... (*To him*) But then? What do you do with them?
P: Then I trans-late them. I slowly erase their face.
W: You take away their significance?
P: I take it away. Then I guide the clean bodies out to where the gate of the Lord's Tabernacle lies.
W: A gate? What happens behind it?
P: (*Laughs*) This I do not know. Nobody knows it. It is in The Beyond. There God's words loose their significance. I only know that later on, they are thrown out at another gate. On that sacred place, I have to await them and pick them up.
W: But if you do not know about the gate of the Tabernacle, how do you know where they are thrown out?

P: Come on, get out now, but quickly. Otherwise I could become very angry, and I would not recommend you to undergo this experience. Get out now, and I promise you that *all* women will get better jobs. And that you will be the Feminist who will be remembered for having achieved that!

W: No, wait! First tell more about this Tabernacle. I do not believe that you really do not know anything.

P: I only have heard some rumors. I have no access to this zone, I am a sacred man and this world out there is controlled by Lucifer and his helpers, the sirens and witches, and all those, who like frontier-guards watch the entrance. All I can do is make human bodies unassailable for them. But the human mind must go through on its own. Perhaps it is a good experience, but I presume it is rather rough. On their track they have to cross the memory of God. Traces and traces of traces. Once they have gone through the gate the way is not difficult to find. Many have travelled it before, everyone follows tracks laid down since the beginning of the world: The Beyond, yes... But I have never been there myself. Someone has told me a little about it. Anyway. I know by experience where the bodies come out into our world again. Here I stand. That is enough.

W: But... I think... it could be that *I* have just been there!

P: Half of you still is! Oh God! Do you understand now why it is so very dangerous? You still are outside of the limit! You have to come in here immediately!

W: Wait, wait! I am on your *boundary*? But you have no idea how wonderful it is! I would like to stay and perhaps explore it a bit... Maybe this would be a good place for supporting Feminism too! Maybe from here one could keep it in suspension, keep it alive!

P: You do not know what you are saying. Meaningless talk: "Explore it a bit"! Man never will know what is Beyond. Where you are, there is no truth!

W: Maybe true! – But maybe not. It is not so important.

P: Why then do you ask at all? I have never had someone as stubborn and yet so difficult to locate as you! (*Emphatically*) The truth is that you are still outside the limits of representation. The truth is that God's word is not there. There is nothing it could refer to. Just moving silence.

W: But we talk, do not we?

P: Talk, ha! I would not call it "talking", such a meaningless conversation with a nobody!

W: Do you really believe the limits of representation are the limits of language? What a narrow mind you have! You live in your second-hand world and believe there is no firstness for you? Here on your boundary, on the line you draw between your God and your Lucifer, here is the place where things are created. Created and recreated in an ongoing transformation. Here it is where your holy words are born! This is why I am here, and that is why I like it. Do you think that words are made in your mind? Here I feel them bubbling through my body, rolling off my tongue. (*Looks at him*) Maybe a man like you you will never understand this. Look: It is not to make you angry, old father, but your order can never be as beautiful as this one!

P: Do not call me old father *again*! I do believe that you are enjoying yourself, but my concerns are wider than just for the moment. I think about history, about what will happen to you in the future and what will happen to society. Society needs words that mark a difference. Clear words it can hold on to, rely on, it does not need bubbling words, (*with irony*) even if they come out of your sweet mouth. It will not be considered sweet for long. Soon it will be called the salivating mouth of a hysteric woman, the dirty toothless mouth of a witch.

W: (*Sticks out her tongue towards him, but he does not see it*) You are a bit pathetic. ... Do you have a handkerchief? (*He hands it to her. She cleans her mouth*) There is something I still do not understand: Let us presume you also did that with me. You sent me on this passage and – let us presume – now you urgently want me to come over and accept this role because you want to bring everything in the right order again, the order of names and words. But why exactly a Feminist? Would not it be enough to be just anybody? To replace somebody who just has died for example. Has someone killed a Feminist?

P: No. But we need *more* Feminists, more women with a certain consciousness. Our society is in crisis. We need more people who will help to improve it! It cannot stay like this!

W: It cannot stay? So you mean that you do not trust in the order of your god? You mean that in fact you are not searching for perfect translations?

P: Perfect translations, perfect translations! Do you know what you are talking about? No translation is perfect, otherwise it would not be a translation!

W: Yes, but what you are doing is much more! You do not care about the stability of society. You change the world through small displacements, small "mistakes"... or maybe bigger "mistakes"...?

P: No. No. Not me...

W: No? Not you? Perhaps someone else. Is there someone who helps you?

P: No! No!

W: Hmm... I think I begin to understand: A little displacement, a little lie: Of course a holy man cannot do this. You must have made a deal with Lucifer. It is the little finger of Lucifer that twists things a bit and moves them...

P: Our society needs to change, otherwise it will destroy itself!

W: I do believe that you have good intentions, but this exactly is your tragedy! (*To herself*) By not undressing his medium totally before the transition act, the guards of Lucifer recognize it and impress the body... And afterwards this priest can impress their mind... Funny, in my case something must have gone wrong. They did touch my mind in this transition, but somehow I did not completely loose my memory. But now I will not let this priest touch my body. (*To him*) Through Lucifer disturbing the body you manipulate the mind, don't you?!

P: Oh God!

W: What do you mean by "Oh God"?! The protector of society as you said? No, you secretly have taken his place! You made the deal with Lucifer and now it is you who has the plan, you who decides about change, and change not for the sake of the stability of society, but change for the sake of the stability of your power.

P: You understand nothing! Look at the world! Do you see the injustice? You are a woman. Do you see these women, do you see these children? They are not as privileged as you are. I had to make this deal. How else could I fight all this evil?

W: So it was for moral reasons!

P: For human reasons!

W: For human reasons, yes. I can understand you very well... But tell me: How do you know in which direction to change the world to be sure that it will become more human?

P: I am the priest!

W: I see. You have to save the world. Of course, as the priest... – Can women become priests as well?

P: Hmm... why not... (*To her with new hope:*) Well, my lady, so far women have not been priests. But maybe there could be... (*Forcefully*) Come over here, I will make you a final offer: You may become a priest, the first of my assistants, and perhaps... perhaps even my successor!

W: Nooo. I rather stay here.

P: But a priest! Think of the power you will have! The power to lead society, and the responsibility! You do not have to be a Feminist, you will be something much more powerful! You will be in a position to change the world in the name of God! My assistant! Think of it!

W: You are dangerous! I do not want to change the world.

P: But it needs to change, just look at it!

W: It needs to change because there are so many who want to change it. You *already* have many assistants! It does not in the least tempt me to be just one more of them. I want to understand the world. And this here is a perfect position for it. I know: When I understand the world a little bit better, then the world will have changed all by itself.

P: Do not tell me you do not want to change the world! What you want is dangerous. From where you are now you could do things far more dangerous than I could even think of!

W: Yes, you are right, but it is a matter of trust.

P: A matter of trust, yes. But how could I trust a nobody? – (*To himself*) But I have no choice: I must take the lesser of the evils. (*To her, officially*) I shall resign. Please come over here now and take my seat – on the right hand of God!

W: (*Looks at him, is silent*)

Lights off.
END

WOMAN AS UTOPIA
Against relations of representation

by Dagmar Reichert[1]

> *In my writing I experience "woman as never completely present and never completely absent, as one who does not have a place to exist, and who cannot turn herself into a subject. (...) And still one would have to say that I, by writing, have in fact turned myself into a man. Perhaps this is where my disorientation comes from, that I am in fact a man, but do not know what a man is and hence do not know what I am. It will probably be a third one, one which I catapult out of myself."*[2]

3. The Archimedean Principle: A body dipped into water is affected by a static buoyancy which is equal to the weight of the amount of water it displaces.
4. Further characteristics:
4.1. Water does not have a form. Rather it tends to transform into an all-encompassing sphere. Dew builds drops, drops flow together, streams form circuits.
4.2. Water builds forms. They emerge in the balance between its tendency towards the sphere and other forces such as gravitation, and result in currents of meanders, waves, or funnel-shaped whirls.

---

1 This text was written in the fall of 1991 and presented at the Basel meeting of the "Deutscher Geographentag 1991".
The four quotes used to separate the different sections of the paper (from "was indistinguishable" to "smooth and shining") stem from Virginia Woolf's book The Waves.
2 Elfride Jelinek in: Das vampirische Zwischenleben, Interview in Die Tageszeitung, Berlin, *9.5.1990.*

Whirls. 4.3. Currents are surfaces, twi-sted planes of water, gliding past each other. They form, where water touches other substances or water of a different speed, composition or temperature Boundary layers react on minimal
    changes in the balance of forces in displacing and
        condensing each other they form resistance without
        solidity, an impulse continues as a wave moving
        over a smooth surface, the dynamic equilibrium
        of a river forms standing waves
        they are shot through by water
        horizontal and vertical currents meet
    and curl up
  forming closed bodies
  pulsating in their particular rhythm
funnels extend and contract the movement gradually balances the differing forces and dissolves them...

Basel, March 15th 1518: A certain, well known scholar, called Erasmus and born in Rotterdam, turns the leaves of an old friend's book. It has just been delivered from the printers, and even though he does not agree completely with everything he now reads there, he still feels that what he holds in his hand could become an important book, perhaps even one that will make history. Name of the author: Thomas More. Name of the book: *Utopia*.

Out of some inner compulsion that book really made history, and although it was not the first book of this kind, it gave its name to a whole series of subsequent works and even to a whole genre: the name "Utopia" was invented by Thomas More as a combination of the Greek adverb *ou* – non – and the substantive *topos* – place.

Utopia, More's non-place is – like Plato's Atlantis[3] – an imaginary island beyond the limits of the old world. But Utopia – alluding to the greek *eutopia* – is also "the happy place", and the name was soon associated with descriptions of a better world and an ideal society, be it a society dominated by authoritarian ideals like that of

---

3 Kritias, Chapter 6, 112 ff. and Timaios, Chapter 3, 25ff..

Plato's *State*, the scientifically organized society Francis Bacon described, or a society based on personal responsibility as in H.G. Wells's imagination[4] or in William Morris's *News from Nowhere*. But it is not these utopias that I intend to write about in describing "woman as utopia", neither will I interpret classical feminist utopias such as *Herland* by Charlotte Perkins Gilman. Much has been written about the different ways in which contemporary social concerns, such as gender relations, were resolved in utopian societies, and much has also been written about the utopias of women authors.[5] This is not surprising, for there is no better way of understanding a society's self-conception than by studying its utopias. As descriptions of non-places, not only do they reflect their culture's most fundamental problems, but they also reveal their deepest taken for granted.[6] Nevertheless, I do not intend to write about women in, or as authors of, utopias, but about woman as utopia. "Woman as utopia" in its double singular form, is not meant to be presumptuous generalization, nor an attempt at unification. It is not some particular woman or utopia I am concerned with here, but the idea of woman and of utopia itself. The idea and its geography.

It would be fascinating for geographical thought to compare history's different utopias. A "geography of utopias" could reveal displacements in the place of non-places and show how they were connected with changing ideas of the shape of the world and with the world's progressive investigation: The utopias of the 17th and 18th

---

4 *In his utopia* Menschen, Göttern gleich.

5 *Apart from* Herland, *the feminist utopias of Sally Gearhart (*Das Wanderland*), Joanna Russ (*The Female Man*), and Marge Piercy (*Women On The Edge Of Time*) also became well known and discussed. See for example Hillary Rose's paper "Dreaming the Future" (1988), in which she writes about both feminist and classical utopias. See also Ulla Zöhrer-Ernst's critique "Von der Sinnenfeindlichkeit utopischer Modelle" (1989) where she refers to Charlotte Perkins Gilman's* Herland. *The creation of ideal images of women and their influence on women's reality is a theme of Christina von Braun's excellent literary analysis in* Die schamlose Schönheit des Vergangenen *(1989).*

6 *See for example Michael Curry's* After nuclear war: Possible Worlds and the Cult of Expertise *(1985), where contemporary scenarios of a world after a nuclear holocaust are used to indicate some things deeply taken for granted in our culture. These can be seen in institutions and modes of behaviour which – as the texts of the scenarios reveal – the authors find difficult to change, even after such an event.*

Centuries were significantly inspired by the discovery of the New World. But in the second half of the 18th Century (Cook had just discovered the Australian east coast), there were no more empty spaces left in the world for non-places, and utopias were transferred onto the dimension of time.[7] Thus the ideal society was situated as a more or less attainable aim[8] on the axis of progress. In our century however, the utopias seem to have transgressed into yet another dimension. A dimension we are already counting on, but are not yet able to name or designate by anything other than that which it is not: not space, but hyperspace, not time, but simultaneity. It may be that this dimension is foreshadowed at the points where it intersects with our usual space-time axes – Tokyo's stock exchange or the third world metropolis, which encompasses all the world's places. Technological development and the increase in trade of signs and goods seem to have unfolded this new dimension which contains white spots for the non-places of today. It is a dimension in which the old striving towards the telos of history, which has lost its place, can find a new direction.

But there is another reason why a geography of utopias is particularly interesting to me. It is because the space it is concerned with is that of the paradox. The paradox is a position which is logically not allowed to exist, because it is, although deduced correctly, contradictory. But although it is logically excluded, this position still takes place; in utopia for example. There are several reasons, why utopia is a paradox. One is that, unlike other texts about fictitious societies, it presupposes that the society it describes exists somewhere already. Somewhere in the nowhere. – And it is due to this paradoxical position that places such as Atlantis, Bensalem, Erewhon, the Sun-state, or Ikarien, are so difficult to map.

In order to map something, it must have a place. A place is a position in an ordering-space, geographical, social, or of whatever kind.

---

7 *There are also some classical utopias which are situated in a non-place in time. It is, however, a place within the cyclical time of a returning golden age. Reinhart Kosseleck (1982, p.1) dates the "jump" into a linear axis of time and the start of temporal utopias in 1770, when Luis-Sebastien Mercier's novel* The year 2440 *was published in France.*

8 *See Ernst Bloch, 1982, vol. 1, chapter 18*

It is a rigid order of solidity that holds sway there, the rigid order of solid things. Its basic rules are:

§1: A=A (axiom of identity)

That which is to be located has to be clearly identifiable. This means that it must not change during the process of localization nor be changed through this process.[9] In addition to this, everything that is to be located has to be measurable on a scale it shares with at least one other thing.

§2: A≠-A (axiom of prohibited contradiction)

There may be empty space, but there cannot be two objects in the same location in space.

§3: A=A v A=B (axiom of excluded third)

That which is to be located must have unequivocal and homogeneous characteristics. It has to have clear and solid boundaries[10], i.e. has to be clearly defined. Thus it will not be mixed with something else nor will there be two different things in one place. Within an occupied location there must be no ambiguous realms. Of each position within the ordering-space, one must be able to determine exactly whether or not it is something's place.

The axioms of logic are the basic rules of mapping, of cartography. Whatever violates these axioms cannot have a place in space; not geographical space, not social space, nor any other order.

Surprisingly perhaps, closer interpretation shows that not even the space of possibility is capable of accommodating utopias. They are too paradoxical for that: there is within every utopia, for example, the inherent contradiction that there is, even at the end of all desire, still something to live towards. When the ideal society is achieved, change is no longer sought for and the journey is over; change has become a meaningless concept. Even so, people in utopian societies do still strive towards things, still hope and fear change, still create.

Thus if the idea of utopia is too paradoxical to be possible, the in-

---

9 This means that the act of locating and the object located have to be strictly separated. Nothing may locate itself. The ordering-space has to be absolutely independent of the elements it orders.

10 They may well have fuzzy boundaries (i.e. be "fuzzy sets"), but ones which can be defined clearly.

tention to write utopia cannot be anything but a paradox: it establishes an ideal society which it can only hope to reach by not adhering to it too rigidly. To allow the utopian possibility of reforming the social, utopian thought must remain open to continuous redefinition. Social reform does not go according to plan or with a fixed apparatus of order. The break-down of Soviet Communism[11] and the tragic outcomes of social engineering's best intentions tell us something about the consequences of neglecting this inherent paradox.

... the water was indistinguishable from the sky, except that it was slightly creased, like a wrinkled cloth. Gradually, as the sky whitened, a dark line lay on the horizon dividing it from the sky, and the grey cloth became barred with thick strokes moving, one after the other, beneath the surface, following each other, pursuing each other, perpetually...

Utopias cannot be located. They are too fluid for topo-logic,[12] nontheless they exist and they work. Reality is more than that which can be defined and located.[13] Reality is also that which gives direction and meaning to our actions. One might say that utopias are a base, but a base without place, a real non-place: non-place as well as a

---

11 But it is certainly not also automatically a break-down of collectivist or Marxist utopias, as some journals recently interpreted it. See for example the headline of the Swiss journal Wochenzeitung *on 12th July 1991: "Leben nach der Utopie". Its argument about the end of utopia implies, as demonstrated by A. Gross (1991, p.107), that there is neither the demand nor the capacity for change.*

12 In *"On boundaries" (1992) I have described the topo-logic and its central role in philosophy in more detail.*

13 In *his world-order Plato distinguished three basic types of being: The "ideal", which can be thought and exists in an ever-unchanging form; the "reproduction" which is visible and is becoming and passing away; and a third, "difficult and dark kind", of which he says that it is taking up all becoming, like a mother. It is not to be perceived and can only be apprehended by "a kind of spurious reason, and (it) is hardly real - which we, beholding as in a dream, say of all existence that it must of necessity be in some place and occupy a space, but that what is neither in heaven nor in earth has no existence. Of these and other things of the same kind, relating to the true and waking reality of nature, we have only this dreamlike sense, and we are unable to (...) determine the truth about them." (Timaios, Kap. 18, 52b.)*

"place", both and neither. And this is why I can speak of "the utopia of woman".

For woman, too, is utopia.

Talking of woman's non-place, I am not just calling for more space for woman, her right to a room of her own, I am not just demanding recognition for her place in society. These changes are necessary, but faced with the consequences of defining a place at all, such demands are not radical enough! It is not enough to draw a "topography of gender" and show that Western tradition locates woman outside culture, in nature, in the wilderness. If Antigone was not understood in the city of Kreon, it was not because her proper place was outside its gates,[14] but because her language could not be located at all. It was because her language was utopian. Is it not written that she had left nothing but traces in the dust, no visible, lasting sign of representation? Antigone is not a subject of representation, and her language, the language of a woman, is not one that could have been laid down in a past. Those who try to do it nevertheless, those who draw a map of the ex-clusion of woman, still work on the basis of our patriarchic culture, our cartographic culture, a culture in which every-"thing", even woman's non-place has to be located, defined, and fixed in its position. It is from the specific perspective of the One, that the Other is territorialized, named and bound.[15] And the One, who turns the Other into an object such that both lose their lifeliness, is the modern subject, traditionally the man. For it is only in relation to that subject that the object exists, She Other, who is judged by his standards.[16] Only in this relation

---

14 As was proposed by Sigrid Weigel (1989, p.10/11). But I take it to be an inexact expression of her, because elsewhere she writes about the problem of "the double place of the woman" (p.261). On the other hand she rejects any characterization of "woman" as undefined, unequivocal and flowing, and thus I wonder if she would not nevertheless disagree.

15 See Sigrid Weigel 1989, p.269.

16 Irigaray calls a woman who defines her identity in such a relation "L'afemme", woman and un-woman, other gender and impossible gender at the same time (eg. 1977, p.112).

she exists, has presence. She is represented by him.[17] Only at the expense of a represented Other can the modern subject hope to gain the security and autonomy it so urgently seeks. Only in this form can it speak of its identity.

Representation characterizes every dualistic subject-object relationship, the presently dominating gender-relations as well as humanity's relation with the environment. Everywhere two characteristics hold:

1. Identity is achieved by delimiting: the Other is that which the One is not. They exclude one another, always remaining in distant contradistinction. Crossing this distance means death of the Self. Man is that which is not nature. And woman? In the mirror of her eyes he recognizes himself.

2. The dualistic subject-object relationship is assymetrical. The One is always the first one, he who was there before, the origin out of whose rib, out of whose looks, out of whose imagination the Other is supposed to receive her identity.[18] It is for this reason that he has to be master and the one who is on top. Relations of representation have their own spatial order.

The more man's self-understanding as Subject grew and the further it spread, the more it became evident that it could not achieve the certainty and autonomy it wanted. Isolated from the Other which endangered its identity while nourishing it, isolated from nature, from woman, from the insane, ... and from utopia, it became

---

[17] *An intelligent and very amusing demonstration of this relation of representation is given by Irigaray in the first chapters of her book* Speculum. *There she dismantles the Freudian theory of female sexuality and of the development of the female child – in a very fair way in fact – and shows to what extent they rely on the norms and function of male sexuality and the development of the male child. For example: In the context of suggesting that for Freud, becoming a woman consists mainly of recognizing and accepting "one's own phallic shortcoming", Irigaray concludes: "A man, minus the ability to (re-)present oneself as a man = a normal woman"(1980, p.30).*

[18] *In her book* Zählen und Erzählen *Eva Meyer demonstrates the possibility of female language and writing as a simultaneous movement behind and beside the identity (the identical subject) of classical logic. She relates to gender relations what G. Günther showed in different myths of creation, namely that the creation of a One, a being capable of reflection, requires a second Other deduced from it. (1983. p.43ff. and 80ff)*

empty.[19] Today it is not only the Subject which is threatened with decay, that which used to be the Object also no longer confines itself to positions of obedient servitude.

For me, a critique of subject-object relations and of man's understanding of its self through these relations seems today even more important. Such a critique would point to the underlying reasons for environmental destruction, the dominating gender relations, and their connection between sex and violence.[20] On the basis of all that, it would uncover a cartographic logic, a logic of place and solid bodies in space, which has gone too far.

In a critique of the topo-logical identity of the modern subject, the interests of feminism and human ecology meet. The ecological questions Francisco Varela or Herbert Spencer Brown have been asking resemble the concerns of feminists like Julia Kristeva or Eva Meyer. Together they question the understanding of the modern Self, in order to open up possibilities for change. For feminists, however, this involves one further problem: how can woman, who has traditionally been the Other, leave (t)his representational position without having to define an Other herself, without having to become a topo-logical subject herself? How can she gain a voice in society and its institutions without being a Subject, without treating other human beings as the Others, and without defining her territory against them? It would be too easy to be satisfied with joining that game and too moderate to be satisfied with a place, blank space, a

---

19 *Julia Kristeva writes: "A 'subject' only exists in a thinking of the sign, which compensates the parallel multiplicity hidden in the semiotic practices of the domination of the sign, by conceding itself 'secondary'- or 'peripheral' phenomena (dream, lyric, madness) that remain subordinated to the sign" (In:* Semiotike. Recherches pour une sèmanalyse, *p.274. Translated after E. Meyer, 1983, p.66).*

20 *In her paper "Herrschaft-Knechtschaft. Die Phantasie von der erotischen Unterwerfung." (1989) J. Benjamin demonstrates, how the presently dominating idea of "rationality" is characterized by a structure of dualistic subject-object relations in just the same way as the presently dominating forms of sexuality. In both cases it results in mutual violence, because such a relation does not allow the vital interplay of openness and closure, dependency and autonomy in each particular person. It only, and with predetermined, fixed distribution, allows it between different persons. The violence, whose logic Benjamin demonstrates in the extreme of sado-masochistic relations, but which also holds for more "normal" relations, arises in the attempt to break free from these predetermined roles.*

few pages. Maintaining here, what her critique of the topo-logical subject demands, is the difficulty, but also – at least for me – the fascination, of being a woman now. It means trying to balance on the tightrope of utopia, moving between the order of place and that of nothing. It is not impossible enough not to try!

... their quivering mackerel sparkling was darkened; they massed themselves; their green hollows deepened and dark might be traversed by shoals of wandering fish. As they splashed and drew back they left a black rim...

So far I have simply assumed it: woman as utopia, non-place. But why should she be? Is it not presumptuous to talk about "woman as utopia"?

I claim that woman is non-place because I am sure that she is more than the relationally represented object, and because I hope that she will be more than the dominating subject.[21] In this assumption I start with myself. While it might be the outer side of the Other that the majority of women come from, I first knew the boundaries of the autonomous subject from the inside, and only later discovered the other possibility. Now I think that both experiences have to come together to challenge and transcend the boundaries of the dominating subject. It yields a "more" which may at first sight appear as less, as a lack of property on the reality market,[22] the "lack" of a human being who has given up solid identity and changes it from one place to the other, forever remaining a nomad, a vagabond perhaps, a woman who does not subject herself to the territorial order, but is not lost in formless chaos either. What a mistake to think she would settle for less!

---

21 *In this respect it is interesting to note that, Theodor Adorno, arguing in another context, writes that "utopia", for him, consists in a "nonidentity of the subject that goes without sacrifice" (1984, p.277).*

22 *See L. Irigaray's paper "Waren untereinander" (1977, p. 199 - 204 and p. 31 ff). There she sketches the economy as an exchange relation based on men's desire of other men (mimetic desire). Heterosexuality would then be a an assignment of roles in this economy: "Men" would be the exchanging subjects, and the "women" would be the goods, objects with an exchange value between men and a use value for them.*

Breaking this self-conception of the modern subject would be as reasonable for men as for women. Why then should it be the woman who should carry this shift? The answer is clear: woman, because she does not fear death! Because woman, it is claimed,[23] does not have to search for the origin by means of the subject, but stands in relation to the past already. Because she knows pleasure, enjoyment, unaware of the singularity of desire.

But fear not! This is not to propose the new super-woman!

The meaning of such assertions may become clearer if they are considered against the background of certain theories of the child's ego-development. I will describe them briefly:

These theories of the children's development of a sense of self are based on the psychoanalytic works of Freud on the one hand, and Saussure's structuralist theory of language on the other. These were brought together, criticised, and further developed by Melanie Klein and by Jacques Lacan in particular, and later in the more or less homogeneous schools which emerged out of their work, by the English representatives of the object relations school[24] and the French post-Lacanian school.

According to these theories, the ego develops as follows[25]: It begins in a contradiction. The newborn child feels its body stimulated which leads to unpleasure. Pleasure, on the other hand, is achieved through the discharge of sensation. Its body does not yet grasp itself, and unites with – or separates from – its environment, the mother's body, depending on the pleasure it receives from it. It has no fixed boundaries. It is thus difficult to name and define, as it is not something for anybody, is nobody. J. Kristeva calls it "Chora" and describes how it is flown through by rhythmical energies, how they glide against each other, transferring their intensities to each other, displacing and condensing them according to (biological and socio-

---

23 Gilles Deleuze, quoted in J. Kristeva, 1978, p.11
24 J. Benjamin (1990, p.220) gives an overview of the contemporary representatives of the theory of object relations.
25 I base this rough description on J. Kristeva and J. Lacan, without, however, using their precise terminology.

historical) forces of coercion.[26] Between the 6th and 18th month, in the so-called "mirror-phase", the growth of the child leads to a qualitative change: the child recognizes its Self in the Other. Encouraged by the outside world's reactions it begins to consider itself as a separate being, limited by the contours of its body, and as such, equipped with a continuous and coherent identity. Although it is not able to control this body, the child identifies with it as "I" and thereby cuts itself off from its past, from the non-contiuous and non-coherent, non-limited Chora, and the flowing connection to the mother. In a later stage of this development, in the so-called "Oedipal phase", this process of separation is completed. Now the child further loosens the tie to the person who nurtures it, and who previously still was the embodiment of the child's satisfaction. In this phase, the ego-development and the differentiation of male and female sexual identity coincide. In a culture like ours, where persons nurturing small children are predominantly women, this is the point, where male and female ego-demarcations begin to differ.[27] To develop its sexual identity, the girl does not have to distance itself as much from the nurturing person, a woman, as the boy. Developing a male sexual identity demands a clearer separation from the mother

---

[26] *This description refers to Freud's passages about the primary processes ("Primärvorgänge") of the unconscious in his* Interpretation of Dreams. *There he talks about "... processes to which the dream-thoughts, previously constructed on rational lines are subjected to in the course of dream-work", and describes them as follows:*
1) the intensities of the individual ideas become capable of discharge en bloc and pass over from one idea to the other, so that certain ideas are formed which are endowed with great intensity (compression or condensation).
2) ..." intermediate ideas", resembling compromises, are constructed under the sway of condensation. ... Composite structures and compromises occur with remarkable frequency when we try to express preconscious thought in speech. They are then regarded as species of "slips of the tongue".
3) The ideas which transfer their intensities to each other stand in the loosest mutual relations. They are linked by associations of a kind that is scorned by our normal thinking and relegated to the use of jokes (in particular associations based on homonyms and verbal similarities).
4) Thoughts which are mutually contradictory make no attempt to do away with each other, but persist side by side. They often combine to form condensations just as though there were no contradictions between them, or arrive at compromises that our conscious thoughts would never tolerate but that are often admitted in our actions." (Freud, 1961, p.483/485)
[27] *See particularly the theses of N. Chodorow, 1986*

(the nurturing woman), which also means a stronger denial of the pre-oedipal Chora. The male "I" defines itself by this separation and hence concentrates the experience of pleasure in its genitals. In our culture such self-conception is not necessary for the development of the female "I".

The emergence of the child's ability to speak is closely linked with this process: with the "I" with which the child learns to address itself, it begins to think of itself in terms of terms, in terms, however, with which it can only address itself because it thereby misses itself to some extent. It misses his past, misses what it used to be before the cut of separation, i.e. the rhythmically pulsating, spatially non-definable Chora. The desire to express itself – and any desire – aims at a suspension and dissolution of this separation.

This description is very rough. It does not specify how ego-development can be explained by means of semiotic concepts of language, sign, and the relationship between signifier and signified. Nor does it mention the differences that exist between the representatives of the various schools in the interpretations of the pre-Oedipal and Oedipal processes of separation[28]. But it may suffice to explain, why it could be claimed that it will be woman who could break the current construction of the modern subject: woman, because she remains closer to the Chora and can therefore remind the solid, sovereign I of the rhythmical flow from which it has separated itself. She, because she can remind the subject, which has learned to recognize itself in the mirror of the Other, that it does not understand it(s)self, and remind the subject that it can never hope to find an origin in the unbroken identity it represents – even if it has to insist on such a hope. Woman can remind the modern subject of another past, of its emergence from contradiction, and she can demonstrate that it will not be able to sustain a whole and pure idea of itself, but must instead recognize that it also owes itself to all the imperfections of the real.[29]

---

28 *The feminist critique of J. Lacan also starts off at this point. See eg. L. Irigaray, 1977, p.121.*
29 *See E. Meyer, 1983, p.42.*

If, therefore, woman knows pleasure, enjoyment, and is unaware of the singularity of desire, then it is for these reasons. She who did not completely cut her Self off from a relationship with the Chora, the mother, and is not Identity, not One – she can experience an enjoyment that is enough in itself[30] and cannot be located. It is an enjoyment of which she knows nothing except the fact that she feels it.[31]

If one claims that the woman does not fear death, it is for that reason too: the loss of self-identity in the Other cannot frighten her, she who in her knowledge of the past remembers the fractures of her Self. She has no solidity to lose.

This woman, who thus lives in connection to her past, is not a subject, but she is not an object either, not a mere Other. She is not negation, but Negativity,[32] an "external being, internal in every identical closure",[33] and as such she acts according to a logic which is wider than topo-logic.[34] Neither is her individuality a closed form that could be located, nor a formless chaos, but – flown through by

---

[30] Julia Kristeva writes that it would perhaps not be mere chance if it were to be woman who did not speak the language of the modern subject and of the society based on it: "Because remaining in her pleasure immediately general and foreign to the singularity of desire, the woman (...) represents the Negative in the homogeneity of society, the eternal 'irony of the community'. Which means (...) that she is concerned with enjoyment (immediate and general), which distinguishes herself from the body (singular, place of desire and pleasure), whereby she knows very well that there is only an enjoyment of the body (singular). Or, said differently, that her knowledge is a knowledge of enjoyment (immediate and general), beyond the pleasure principle (the pleasure of the body, and be it perverse). Thus her problem is not the fear of death – because she has nothing to be castrated – but rather how to maintain this enjoyment as more than enjoyment or absence of enjoyment, before it turns into a value or an object, ie. before it comes to a stop."(In: Matiäre, sens, dialectique. Translated after E. Meyer, 1983, p.41.)

[31] In "Gott und das Genießen der Frau" Jacques Lacan writes: "There is an enjoyment for her, for this her that does not exist and does not mean anything. There is an enjoyment for her, of which she herself might perhaps not know anything apart from the fact that she feels it – and that, that she knows" (1989, p.81)

[32] This is a distinction J. Kristeva makes and describes in her book Die Revolution der poetischen Sprache.

[33] J. Kristeva, 1978, p.27

[34] Julia Kristeva and Eva Meyer call the woman the "zerological subject", the "subject zero which is nobody, because it annuls itself in a praxis that does not subject itself to the sign" (Meyer, 1983, p.66).

intensities – is always in the process of formation, of building forms out of its relatedness. Neither is she place, nor nothing, but rather non-place, utopia.

But.

... they broke and spread their waters swiftly over the shore. One after another they massed themselves and fell; the spray tossed itself back with the energy of their fall. They were steeped deep-blue save for a pattern of diamond-pointed light on their backs which rippled as the backs of great horses ripple with muscles as they move. They fell; withdrew and fell again, like the thud of a great beast stamping...

But. Such a woman? Such should a woman be? Should a woman be such? Is this not dream rather than utopia? Is this not yet another attempt to pin woman down to a new ideal, to place her once more? To identify her as a "non-place" this time, as the "ship which, with its white sails, like an immense butterfly, passes over the dark sea"? Once more woman as the "calm enchanting being" which the "man in the midst of his hubbub, in the midst of the breakers of his plots and plans (...) sees gliding past him, (and) for whose happiness and retirement he longs"[35] – and this time not only man, but the self-imprisoned modern subject in general?

This criticism is frequent, but it fails. No. Calling her "utopia" and "non-place" I am not simply defining and locating woman yet again. This is important, and there are two reasons for claiming it:

The first one is that this text is not about anything, but it is itself what it is. If it has to be about something at all, it is at the most about mere tautologies[36]. If it is correct that woman is utopia, then I have not said anything other than "utopia is utopia", or that "woman stands in closer relation to the Chora" because she who stands in

---

35 F. Nietzsche, Fröhliche Wissenschaft, *Kap. 60/20ff.*
36 See Wittgenstein's definition of meaningful assertions in the Tractatus.

closer relation to the Chora is a woman. A woman is a woman. (And not a rose.)

Tautologies do not tell us anything about the world. They represent nothing. And I shall take good care not to represent! Certainly not quietly, by counting on a silent agreement on social conventions, blinking with an eye "well, we all know who belongs to us women, don't we?" But apart from that, there is no one I could tell anything about. This is the second reason: I could not characterize anybody as a woman or utopia in the way I have done, because I would immediately contradict myself. If being a woman means being in a non-place, I cannot lay down this non-place to put a particular person there. It is not solid enough for that. Neither can I tie the word "woman" to where I presume a woman to be, to a non-place: no places to lay down, no one to tie. Time beyond representation.

But if you like, you can take this self as yours and go with it.

Luce Irigaray once said that the point should not be to "develop a new theory, whose subject or object would be the woman, but rather to put a stop to the theoretical machine and suspend its claim of a far too unequivocal truth and a far too unequivocal meaning".[37] Hence I stick to my tautology and insist that I am doing nothing but writing myself. I write this as a woman, and if the woman is utopia she cannot be described, but she can try to be it in the course of reading and writing. This is my utopia, the utopia of a woman.

... they no longer visited the further pools or reached the dotted black line which lay irregularly on the beach. The sand was pearl white, smooth and shining...

37 L. Irigaray, 1977, p.225

References

Acker C, 1990 *In Memoriam to Identity* (Grove Weidenfeld, New York)

Adorno Th, 1984 *Negative Dialektik* (Suhrkamp, Frankfurt)

Bacon F, 1982 *Neu Atlantis* (Reclam, Stuttgart)

Benhabib S, 1986 *Critique, Norm and Utopia: A study of the Foundations of Critical Theory* (Columbia University Press, New York)

Benjamin J, 1989, "Herrschaft – Knechtschaft. Die Phantasie von der erotischen Unterwerfung", in *Denkverhältnisse*. Eds E List, H Studer (Suhrkamp, Frankfurt) pp 511-538

Benjamin J, 1990 *Die Fesseln der Liebe* (Stroemfeld/Roter Stern, Basel)

Berneri M L, 1982 *Reise durch Utopia* (Kramer, Berlin)

Bloch E, 1982 *Das Prinzip Hoffnung* Bd. 1-3 (Suhrkamp, Frankfurt)

Borch-Jacobson M, 1991 *Lacan. The Absolute Master* (Stanford University Press, Stanford)

Chodorow N, 1986 *Das Erbe der Mütter* (Verlag Frauenoffensive, München)

Derrida J, 1979 *Spurs/Eperons* (University of Chicago Press, Chicago)

Deuber-Mankowsky A, 1991,"Weibliches Interesse an Moral und Erkenntnis", in *Denken der Geschlechterdifferenz* Eds H Nagl-Docekal, H Pauer-Studer (Wiener Frauenverlag, Wien), pp 3-12

Foucault M, 1967,"Andere Räume" in: *Aisthesis* Ed K. Barck. (Reclam, Leipzig) pp.34-46.

Frank M, Raulet G, Van Reijen W, 1988 *Die Frage nach dem Subjekt* (Suhrkamp, Frankfurt)

Gearhart S, 1982 *Das Wanderland* (Verlag Frauenoffensive, Wien)

Gilman Perkins Ch, 1979 *Herland* (Random House, New York)

Günther G, 1980 *Beiträge zu einer operationsfähigen Dialektik* Band 3 (Meiner, Hamburg)

Goodey B, 1970, "Mapping Utopia" *The Geographical Review* 60 15-30

Gross A, 1991, "Über das Geschäft mit der unechten Zukunft", in *Werbung ist für alle da* Eds M Heller, W Keller (Museum für Gestaltung, Zürich) pp 106-116.

Hrachovec H, 1980 *Vorbei. Heidegger, Frege, Wittgenstein. Vier Versuche* (Stromfeld/Roter Stern, Basel)

Irigaray L, 1977 *Das Geschlecht das nicht eins ist* (Merve, Berlin)

Irigaray L, 1980 *Speculum. Spiegel des anderen Geschlechts* (Suhrkamp, Frankfurt)

Irigaray L, 1987, "Eine andere Kunst des Geniessens", in *Zur Geschlechterdifferenz* Ed L Irigaray (Wiener Frauenverlag, Wien) pp 17-42

Jameson F, 1986, "Postmoderne – zur Logik der Kultur im Spätkapitalismus", in *Postmoderne* Eds A Huyssen, K Scherpe (Rowohlt, Reinbek) pp 45-102.

Koselleck R, 1982, "Die Verzeitlichung der Utopie", in *Utopieforschung*, Bd. 3 Ed W Voßkamp (Metzler, Stuttgart) pp 1-14

Kristeva J, 1978 *Die Revolution der poetischen Sprache* (Suhrkamp, Frankfurt)

Lacan J, 1986 *Encore (Seminar XX)* (Quadriga, Berlin)

Lacan J, 1987 *Die 4 Grundbegriffe der Psychoanalyse (Seminar XI)* (Quadriga, Berlin)

Lechte J, 1990 *J. Kristeva* (Routlege, London)

Mauss M, 1989, "Der Begriff der Person und des Ich.", in *Soziologie und Anthropologie, Vol 2* Ed M Mauss (Fischer, Frankfurt) pp 221-252

Merchant C, 1987 *Der Tod der Natur* (Beck, München)

Meyer E, 1983 *Zählen und Erzählen. Für eine Semiotik des Weiblichen* (Medusa, Wien)

Meyer E, 1990 *Der Unterschied, der eine Umgebung schafft: Kybernetik, Psychoanalyse, Feminismus* (Turia u. Kant, Wien)

Moi T, 1986 *The Kristeva Reader* (Basil Blackwell, Oxford)

More Th, 1989 *Utopia* Ed G Logan, R Adams (Cambridge University Press, Cambridge)

Nicholson L, 1990 *Feminism/Postmodernism* (Routledge, New York)

Nietzsche F, 1988 *Fröhliche Wissenschaft* Krit. Studienausgabe, Bd. 3 (dtv/de Gruyter, München)

Piercy M, 1979 *Women at the Edge of Time* (Woman's press, London)

Platon, 1959 *Kritias* Sämtliche Werke Bd. 5 (Rowohlt, Hamburg)

Platon, 1959 *Timaios* Sämtliche Werke Bd. 5. (Rowohlt, Hamburg)

Reichert D, 1992, "On boundaries" *Society and Space* 10 pp 87-98

Riley D, 1988 *Am I that Name? Feminism and the Category of "Women" in History* (University of Minnesota Press, Minneapolis)

Rose H, 1988, "Dreaming the Future" *Hypatia*, Vol. 1, 1988, pp.119-138

Russ J, 1985 *The Female Man* (Woman's press, London)

Schwenk Th, 1988 *Das sensible Chaos.* (Verlag freies Geistesleben, Stuttgart)

Spencer Brown G, 1969 *The Laws of Form* (Allen and Unwin, London)

Varela F, 1975, "A calculus for self-reference" *International Journal of General Systems* 2 pp 2-24

Von Braun Ch, 1989 *Die schamlose Schönheit des Vergangenen* (Verlag Neue Kritik, Frankfurt)

Voßkamp W, 1982 *Utopieforschung* 3 Bände (Metzler, Stuttgart)

Weigel S, 1990 *Topographien der Geschlechter* (Rowohlt, Reinbek)

Woolf V, 1931 *The Waves* (Hogarth Press, London)

Zöhrer-Ernst U, 1989, "Von der Sinnenfeindlichkeit utopischer Modelle", in *Die Revolution hat nicht stattgefunden* (Diskord, Tübingen) pp 187-198

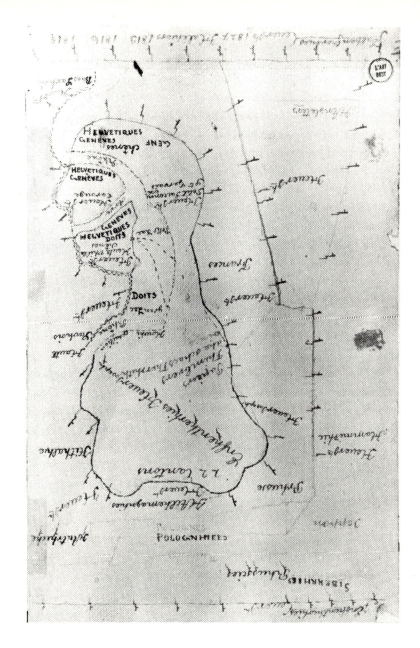

Josef Heuer: Buste composé en carte de suisse

THE FORM OF RELATEDNESS

by Mario Neve

> To make the unexpected as it is expected, in such a way we can stimulate the evolution of things, avoiding, on the one hand, the pool of the well-known, and on the other the wandering of randomness. In such a way, Sir, art and science have the same requirements and dignity.
>
> J.S. Bach (Letter to I. Newton, december 1719)

Aria

Biological life is born at first blow. Social life needs a second round. Man is not able to accept life in its nakedness, the "absolutism of reality" (Blumenberg, 1979a): human beings cannot keep in touch with reality because reality is the realm of Becoming, i.e. of unpredictability. The unexpected in turn gives birth to anxiety (*Angst*) which is the horizon from which something can come.

The process of hominization – that is to say the birth of culture – creates an *inner distance* that separates instinct from action, allowing eventually the rise of "second-order thinking" (Elkana, 1986) in which "the production of material artifacts without the concomitant production of linguistic artifacts, and conversely, is not even *thinkable*".[1] Of course, *representation* – as second-order thinking in a strict sense – shows itself not only as a defensive device, a *déplacement* which removes the hard contact with reality, but also as a powerful way to rule the Becoming: "Foreseeing means that the becoming (the time, the history) has to fit itself into the foreseen order; but such an order has to be unchanging, for otherwise the

---

1 Rossi-Landi, 1985, p.48

threat of the becoming is again turned into a real possibility".[2]

The "foreseen order" is nothing but a refined product of the basic device of *déplacement*; a great machinery to create *doubles* of the real, a machinery which comes from the *logos* of Greek thinking. To illustrate how such a shifting occurs, there is a short story from the Golden Age of Greek thought.

During the Peloponnesian War, Pericles is on the verge of laying siege to the town of Epidaurus when, suddenly, the sky is obscured by an eclipse. Everybody is struck with terror and in particular Pericles's helmsman, who goes mad. Pericles saves his ship by covering the head of the helmsman with his own cloak and by asking him if he still feels a terrible calamity or its omen.

Representation works like Pericles's cloak: it is a veil which not only *protects* us against the hardness of reality but also provides us with a *double* of reality, a double which in turn manages our way of thinking. We can define that doubling device as *mapping* (Neve, 1989) or as *cartographical reductionism* (Neve, 1992), but here I shall prefer the term *mediation*.[3]

To follow the theme of mediation as the logical operator of mapping, it is necessary to consider the various arrangements of second-order thinkings in the history of the concept of *Neuzeit*: "The connection between an historically-determinate set of problems and predicaments, and a given set of collective interventions, is mediated by definite forms of discourse. Presumably, this means that the forms of discourse bear some discoverable relationship to the concrete social moments between which they come to life".[4]

But, on the other hand, we must also take into account the so-called *low* forms of knowledge, for instance, various types of behaviour involving human struggles against life's uncertainties observable in situations of crisis and social change. A good example can be found in 17th century England, when merchants, judges,

---

2 *Severino, 1979, p.17*
3 *With regard to such a perspective I have found useful points of view and suggestions in Weber, 1922; Simmel, 1908, Parsons, 1937 and 1951; Luhmann, 1975 and 1984; Girard, 1961 and 1978; Jensen, 1990; Bertelli (ed.), 1992.*
4 *Scott, 1982, p.145*

carpenters, travellers and surveyors experienced a new approach to reality that influenced the scientific theories of Boyle and Newton (Gargani, 1975).

In unfolding such a net it is necessary to use a multifocal sight in order to connect different manifestations of mapping, such as the foundation of a new order of the world based upon *measure* and *computing* (Koyré, 1961), the evolution of writing (Ong, 1982; Goody, 1977, 1986, 1987; Havelock, 1978), the transition in scientific thought from the *substance-concept* (*Substanzbegriff*) to the *function-concept* (*Funktionsbegriff*) (Cassirer, 1910), the evolution of *mnemonics* (Rossi, 1960) and Artificial Intelligence (Minsky, 1985), etc.

The theme of the present paper is an *Übergang*, a transition phase in the instituted process whereby social mediation is based upon an homogeneous spatial structure. This is the birth of the modern State. Its starting-point is the 17th century and the work of a philosopher whose thought deeply influenced the development of modern science: R. Descartes (1596-1650). Following the spirit of the baroque age and the rules of counterpoint[5] we will connect Cartesian thinking with the voice of G.W. Leibniz (1646-1716).

Variatio 1

> *Mens potest plura simul cogitare.*
> *Mens igitur potest per operationem in pluribus locis esse.*
>
> G.W. Leibniz

In his *Regulae ad directionem ingenii* (*Rules to Orient the Intelligence*, 1628) Descartes defines *intuition* and *deduction* as the only ways to obtain "clear and distinct thoughts". While deduction is described as an argumentative chain whose basic quality is *clear-*

---

5 *The idea of science as dreamed by Leibniz and the idea of geography as dreamed by myself have the same root: the language of music. But this is the subject-matter of another essay on which I am working.*

ness, intuition is defined by Descartes through the use of four examples: "Then everybody can perceive by intuition that he exists, that he thinks, that the triangle is limited by three lines, the ball by one surface, and so on" (*Regula* III).

The order of examples is not incidental – as notes Michel Serres – but establishes a link between the order of *pure intuition* (being, thinking) on the one hand, and the order of *spatial intuition* (triangle, ball), on the other hand. Such links do not belong to the realm of traditional deduction because they are part of an *inter-intuitive* order. Both the first and the second set of examples is ruled by *necessity* and *sufficiency* but the objects of the second are not geometrical figures; Descartes says ball (*globum*) not sphere.

We have here an argument which admits important consequences. In fact there is not only an *isomorphism* between the arrangements of the two kinds of intuition, but, if we reorganize the text of the *Regula* according to the logical series (thinking *before* being, line *before* triangle, surface *before* ball), we find another important isomorphism with the famous "Ego cogito, ergo sum, sive existo" ("I think, then I am, i.e. I exist") of the 4th part of the *Discourse on Method* (1637). The relation between *being* and *thinking* allowed by the mediation of *ergo* is therefore inter-intuitive, i.e. it belongs to the realm of absolute *a priori*.

The *ergo* is an *operator* which is absolutely a priori as to every deduction: it is the *ergo* which makes possible the link between the two orders, it is the *mediator* that guarantees the communication, the *translator* between two orders of language. It does not work according to geometry or mathematics but in accordance with "an analogy of behaviour based on necessity and sufficiency".[6] It is a model that operates by means of an analogical symmetry.

To grasp the importance of such a translation it is necessary to consider the Cartesian discourse in its relations with the Leibnizian universe.

In fact, if Descartes affirms that space is equivalent to *extension* establishing, at the same time, its conditions of *existence*, Leibniz

---

6 Serres, 1968, p.118

states that space is *ordo cohexistendi* (the order of co-existences, in the sense of what co-exists *as possibility*) but *it does not exist*: space neither exists nor will exist, because it is "the *law* of what will happen".[7]

Leibnizian space is not determined as from a fixed point, i.e. the *subject* (like in linear perspective, the relation with the object of the Cartesian model). Instead it is the subject itself which is determined by its localization in a point of view by a given *situs* (place) and a given moment: "it is not a variation of truth as from the subject, but it is the condition which lets the subject see the truth of a variation. It is the same concept as the baroque perspective".[8]

In this sense, space is the *milieu* of intersections in which beings take place. The form of such intersections, i.e. their arrangement, is always *cultural* (Serres, 1977). What we name culture is the arranger that adapts the intersections to a new order whose representation is multidimensional and shows all possible (i.e. legal) paths: an orchestral score.

Such a conception, with all its relativism, makes clearer the consequences of the Cartesian translator.

We stated, at the beginning of the present paper, that the birth of man as cultural being needs the creation of an *inner distance* between instinct and action to avoid constant contact with reality. To Descartes (9th *Regula*) the model of intuition is *vision*. However, sight needs both *light*, as medium, and *distance* from the object to obtain *clear* knowledge.

Now, Descartes's insistence on the method *per imitationem* - analogical - (8th *Regula*) points out the presence, in the more critical passages of the Cartesian works, of the mediating machine: the act of intuition is the *double* of the act of vision. But, since clear knowledge needs an *im-mediate* vision, another double is created: touching as the model of vision. The character of immediateness of touch solves the problem of distance by means of the "model of model": "And then, *intueri* is to see, but it is to see like one touches,

---

7 Belaval, 1976, p. 213
8 Deleuze, 1988, it. tr., p.29

with the abolition of distance and mouvement".⁹

It is important to pay attention to the fact that Leibniz, with his God as guarantor of communication, knows well that "what I connect in the intuition, are not ideas, but only, after their separated conception, their signs or characters".¹⁰ That is to say their re-presentations. Descartes, on the contrary, hides the relativism of his system behind the device of doubling that turns a logical principle from a *right* into a *fact*.

From this device comes "the reduction of matter to pure spatiality"¹¹ that is the conception of space which, after the work of Gassendi and the great Newtonian synthesis, becomes *physicalist space*: the space as measure and computing.

The making of physicalist space reveals the ideological character of the process. In fact, the effectiveness of such a spatial conception in the technical age is determined by its adoption as the unique, truthful representation of life's space (Farinelli, 1985).

Moreover, the representation of one possible space as the only one points to the essence of our argument, on the birth of an homogeneous spatial structure (absolutely fictional) based upon a radical use of mediation's device.

The best proof is the existence of a translation similar to the one we analysed in relation to the Cartesian model.

In that model the *ergo*, a logical operator, becomes the mediator between the order of pure intuition and that of spatial intuition, and here we have another mediator, mapping, which translates the properties of physicalist space (isotropy, homogeneity, continuity) in a new order, i.e. the "neutral" urban space of contemporary cities (Sennett, 1990).

Of course, we must pay attention to the term "contemporary city". Here it means the product of another translation, that of North American urban centres of the 19th century whose model of the *grid* progressively attracted also European urban planning.

---

9 *Serres, 1968,, p.125*
10 *Belaval, 1960, p.267*
11 *Borkenau, 1934, it. tr., p.350*

The urban grid represents the geometric projection of physicalist space *on* life's space. The character of the logical mapping operator reveals itself just in its *neutrality*, both with regards to the method and to the outcomes: it does not matter which urban culture manages such spatial models – the culture of imperial Roman law[12] or the rules of landed property and real estate – because the grid guarantees, though in different contexts of value, the effectiveness of a spatial structure that neutralizes differences.

But to understand this point it is necessary to go back to the achievement of the physicalist conception in the 17th century.

Variatio 2

> *Communemque prius, ceu lumina solis et auras,*
> *Cautus humum longo signavit limite mensor.*
>
> Ovidio, *Metamorphoses, I, 135-6*

With P. Gassendi (1592-1655) we have both a critical judgement on the Cartesian system and the acceptance of its subjectivism. In other words, Gassendi agrees with Descartes in relation to the fundamental position (in the strict sense of a "presence which founds") of the subject in the system. Also in Gassendi we find the metaphysics of the subject as in all modern science, that metaphysics of co-ordinates which Hermann Weyl said was the necessary remainder of the extinction of ego.[13]

But Gassendi solved another problem too, a problem that, once solved, allowed the working out of the concept of absolute space: the question of *horror vacui* (Jammer, 1954).

---

[12] *In spite of Sennet's opinion (Sennett, 1990, it. tr., p.59) the Roman grid is the geometric projection of Roman law and not a way to make Roman soldiers feeling at home all over the world (in relation to this theme see Neve, 1991). It is worth noting that Rome's form is quite different from such a model and this is a further proof that the grid is not a projection by analogy but a result of metaphysical (legal) operations*

[13] *Weyl, 1949, p.75*

This question is very old and its constant presence in Greek and Christian thought is a mark of its essential character. In fact, at the beginning of our paper we noted the Fear of the Becoming as the origin of mediation, but, in a wide sense, we can now define it as the will to give a determined sense to the *nothing*, because (and this attitude is present throughout the Greek and Christian tradition with many modulations): "every history, every time, every becoming and every freedom have to conform to the incontrovertible sense of the whole. In this way, all that has not come yet from the nothing is anticipated and pre-contained, with regard to what it is in truth, in the incontrovertible knowledge".[14]

It is emblematic to note that, in the history of science, the concept of the mathematical *infinite* comes from the concept of the mathematical *nothing*[15] (Rotman, 1987).

With Newton's *Philosophiae naturalis principia mathematica* (1686-1687) the possibility *to imagine* an empty space becomes reality: accepting from Patrizi, Campanella and Gassendi the concept of an infinite, homogeneous and isotropic space, Newton gives birth to the most powerful double of modern thought: the space of classical physics.

On the other hand, the deep transformation of European consciousness which was caused by the geographical discoveries in the 16th and 17th centuries provided an empirical and formal closing for the question. The New World becomes the projective plan on which one can translate the new model of the World: the *horror vacui* is overcome, because the whole Earth becomes visible and recognizable (as measurable) through the double of Newtonian space. This is a great spatial revolution, the first, that grasps *Erde und Welt* (Earth and World) (Schmitt, 1942).

Speaking about this age with regard to the connection between geographical discoveries and the birth of modern states, C. Schmitt recognizes the essence of such State-conception in the character of

---

14 Severino, 1980, p.46
15 On this theme I wrote a forthcoming essay on the infinite, perspective geometry, causality and town-planning between the 17th and 18th century in Europe.

the Christian Empire: "The essential character of the Christian Empire was not to be an eternal kingdom, but to remember always its end (...) and in spite of all to be able to exercise historical power. The decisive and historically important concept at the basis of its continuance was that of the 'restraining force', of *kat-echon*. 'Empire' means here the historical power which is able to *hold back* the advent of Antichrist".[16]

State is the guarantor of safety and communication inside its boundaries, because its space is based upon scientific certainty, that is to say the certainty of physicalist space (Farinelli, 1985). *Katechon* is nothing but the mediating double of *legitimacy* (Neve, 1992), built up by means of *Messung* (survey). It is the legal title (*rectum-Recht-right*) C. Schmitt mentions with regard to the legitimacy of geographical discoveries: in this sense *discovering* is equal to *mapping*, because legitimacy is guaranteed by the representation's certainty.[17]

Of course, this is the origin of the application of grid models to the New World: from the foundation of missionaries and Spanish towns during the age of *Conquistadores* to the *Land Ordinance* by Thomas Jefferson (1785), the neutral, impassive nature of perspective's grid allowed the universal translation (Sica, 1981).

Neither the kind of urban culture that manages space, nor even the spiritual foundation of such a culture do matter: Both, Catholics and Protestants used the same device to rule an unknown space which they considered as a hostile environment. They transformed it into a territory, a political dominion (*Gebiet*).[18]

Schmitt quotes Mackinder, the geographer, in his acknowledgements, but his source is another and more radical: "The State is an organism not only because it constitutes a relation between living people and steady ground (*Boden*), but because such a relation becomes so grounded by means of their inter-action; both become one and it becomes impossible to think of them separatedly without

---

16 Schmitt, 1950, it. tr., p.43
17 Schmitt, 1950, it. tr., p.150
18 see Neve, 1992, p.328

taking life itself away".[19]

And again: "The stronger food and dwelling bind society to its ground, the more urgent becomes society's need to hold on to it. In its essence the State's duty with respect to the ground always remains the same: protection".[20] The nature of the state is evident here: all relations inside its boundaries are political, and their arrangements are conflictual.

It is hard to describe more clearly the "neutralization" of Becoming which is at the basis of the modern state.

Aria da capo

In fine videbitur cuius toni.

M. Luther

In a wide sense we can state that mediation, as the spatial form of human relatedness, always has taken many different degrees of modulation.

The cultural formation which we call Modernity, however, determined a typical way to develop such a model by *dematerializing* the mediator: the *value* of desire is not produced in relation to objects but to models (Girard, 1961 and 1978).

In such a system, power, with its fluctuations of conflict and protection, is able to manage the manipulation of meanings.

Within the state, the political translation of Modernity, the existence of a human being depends on a model: the model of *person*. In fact 'person' comes from *persona* – in Latin language 'mask' – that is the legal fiction which allowed the making of the modern state on the basis of the political conception of *people* as a solution to the problem of the One and the Many (Kantorowicz, 1957 and Neve, 1989). It is the space of the state, as society,[21] which maps my body

---

19 *My translation from Ratzel, 1923, p.4*
20 *My translation from Ratzel, 1899, p.69*
21 *Regarding to the old question about the conflict between state and civil society (Koselleck, 1959), I think that the late events in the EC - and particularly in Germany,*

and gives me the character of a legal person: "The individual will be social or will not be".[22]

Moreover, since Newtonian space became the space of economic relations and the political economy invented the hundredth *double*, the *homo oeconomicus*, politics as the peculiar expression of the State depended on fluctuations in the economic world (Polanyi, 1944).

Political subjects, searching for legitimacy within the State, are confronted with the mediating model which turns a *value* into an *evaluated* (Cacciari, 1991), reducing the living space of relatedness to a consciousness more and more threatened (Sennett, 1990).

The forgetfulness of our origin, the infinite distance from the birth of mankind (Rossi, 1979), increases the difference between *Lebenszeit* (life-time) and *Weltzeit* (world-time) (Blumenberg). Our consciousness lives on two different *scales* and the present time is really *vergangene Zukunft* (past future) (Koselleck, 1979) in which every experience becomes a simulacrum.

The awareness of such a condition is a heavy burden for our generation, but I think that the multifocal perspectives of the present book are a first step towards a change. In a sense, these perspectives are not lonely voices, but are arranged on a large score with many instruments. Hence, we may dare to distrust representation and all its doubles. We may dare the wisdom of Prince Sigismund in *La vida es sueño* by Calderon (III, 1026-1036), whose salvation comes from his distrust, and who thus differed from his father, the King, who trusted in the power of predictability.

This is the challenge. And such is the model we have to grasp in all its implications if we are to accomplish geography's task: to search "the realm of sense of the Earth".[23]

In this sense, and only in this sense, truth will set us free.

France and Italy with all their aspects of xenophobia or bribery - are not a revenge of society over the state, but only a new definition of roles within the state which in turn, in such a process, reveals its frailty.

22 Rosset, 1984, p.116

23 Schmitt, 1950, it. tr., p.15

References

Belaval Y, 1960 *Leibniz critique de Descartes* (Gallimard, Paris)
Belaval Y, 1976 *Etudes leibniziennes* (Gallimard, Paris)
Bertelli S, 1992 *La mediazione* (Ponte alle Grazie, Firenze)
Blumenberg H, 1979a *Arbeit am Mythos* (Suhrkamp, Frankfurt am Main)
Blumenberg H, 1979b *Schiffbruch mit Zuschauer* (Suhrkamp, Frankfurt am Main)
Borkenau F, 1934 *Der Übergang vom feudalen zum bürgerlichen Weltbild* (Wissenschaftliche Buchgesellschaft, Darmstadt). Italian translation: Il Mulino, Bologna, 1984
Cacciari M, 1991, "Carl Schmitt e lo Stato", *La Rivista dei Libri* I/9 12-15
Cassirer E, 1902 *Leibniz' System in seinen wissenschaftlichen Grundlagen* (Elwert, Marburg)
Cassirer E, 1910 *Substanzbegriff und Funktionsbegriff* (Duncker & Humblot, Berlin)
Deleuze G, 1988 *Le pli. Leibniz et le Baroque* (Minuit, Paris; it. tr., Einaudi, Torino, 1990)
Descartes R , 1959 (original 1628) *Regulae ad directionem ingenii*, ed Gouhier (Vrin , Paris)
Elkana Y, 1986 *Anthropologie des Erkenntnis* (Suhrkamp, Frankfurt am Main)
Farinelli F, 1985, "Der Kampf ums Dasein als ein Kampf um Raum: teoria e misura dello spazio geografico dal Settecento ai giorni nostri", in *Geografia per il principe* Ed P Paganini (Unicopli, Milano)
Gargani A, 1975 *Il sapere senza fondamenti* (Einaudi, Torino)
Girard R, 1961 *Mensonge romantique et vérité romanesque* (Grasset, Paris)
Girard R, 1978 *Des choses cachées depuis la fondation du monde* (Grasset & Fasquelle, Paris)
Goody J , 1977 *The Domestication of the Savage Mind* (Cambridge University Press, Cambridge)
Goody J, 1986 *The Logic of Writing and the Organization of Society*, (Cambridge University Press, Cambridge)
Goody J, 1987 *The Interface Between the Written and the Oral* (Cambridge University Press, Cambridge)
Havelock E A, 1978 *The Greek Concept of Justice: From its Shadow in Homer to its Substance in Plato* (Harvard University Press, Cambridge, Mass.)
Jammer M, 1954 *The History of Theories of Space in Physics* (Harvard University Press, Cambridge, Mass.)
Jensen O M, 1990 *The Lord's Tabernacle*, Kappel am Albis, manuscript, now printed as "Herrens Tabernakel" *Norplans Meddelande*, 1991:1
Kantorowicz E H, 1957 *The King's two Bodies. A Study in Medioeval Political Theology* (Princeton University Press, Princeton, N.Y.)

Koselleck R, 1959 *Kritik und Krise* (Karl Alber, Freiburg-München)

Koselleck R, 1979 *Vergangene Zukunft* (Suhrkamp, Frankfurt am Main)

Koyré A, 1961, Du monde de l'«à-peu-près» à l'univers de la precision, in *Études d'histoire de la pensée philosophique* (Colin, Paris)

Leibniz G W,1986 (original 1686) *Discours de métaphysique*, n.e., H Lestienne ed (Vrin, Paris)

Leibniz G W, 1930 (original 1714) *Principes de philosophie ou la Monadologie* Ed E Boutroux (PUF, Paris)

Luhmann N, 1975 *Macht* (Ferdinand Enke Verlag, Stuttgart)

Luhmann N, 1984 *Soziale Systeme* (Suhrkamp, Frankfurt am Main)

Marejko J, 1989 *Cosmologie et politique* (L'Age d'Homme, Lausanne)

Minsky M, 1985 *The Society of Mind* (Minsky, New York)

Neve M, 1987, "Critical Notes on the Concept of Mapping", paper presented at the 5th Colloquium of Quantitative and Theoretical Geography, Bardonecchia, Italy, available as a mimeo from the author

Neve M, 1989, "The Gordian Knot: Steps to an Overcoming of Mapping", in *Les langages des représentations géographiques* Ed G Zanetto (EST, Venezia) pp 293-329

Neve M, 1992, "Legittimità e leggibilità del mondo: note sul Limite come fondamento della rappresentazione", in *Paysage et crise de la lisibilité Eds* L Mondada, F Panese, O Söderstrom, (Institut de Géographie de l'Université, Lausanne), pp 319-333

Neve M, Santoro F A , 1989 *Il Teatro della Memoria* (Fasano, Schena)

Ong W J, 1982 *Orality and Literacy* (Methuen, London & New York)

Parsons T, 1937, 1949 *The Structure of Social Action* (Free Press of Glencoe, New York)

Parsons T, 1951, *The Social System* (Free Press of Glencoe, New York, I Ill)

Polanyi K, 1944, *The Great Transformation* (Holt, Rinehart & Winston, New York)

Ratzel F, 1923 (original 1897) *Politische Geographie* (Oldenbourg, München u. Berlin)

Ratzel F, 1899 *Anthropogeographie I* (Engelhorn Stuttgart)

Rosset C, 1984 *Le réel et son double* (Gallimard, Paris)

Rossi P, 1960 *Clavis Universalis* (Ricciardi, Roma-Napoli)

Rossi P, 1979 *I segni del tempo* (Feltrinelli, Milano)

Rotman B, 1987 *Signifying Nothing* (Macmillan, London)

Schmitt C, 1942, 1981 *Land und Meer*, (Hohenheim Verlag, Köln-Lövenich)

Schmitt C, 1950 *Der Nomos der Erde im Völkerrecht des Jus Publicum Europaeum* (Greven Verlag, Köln). Italian translation: Adelphi, Milano 1991

Scott A J, 1982, "The meaning and social origins of discourse on the spatial foundations of society", in *A Search for Common Ground* Eds P R Gould and G Olsson (Pion, London)

Sennett R, 1990 *The Conscience of the Eye. The Design and Social Life of Cities* (Alfred A Knopf, New York). Italian translation: Feltrinelli, Milano 1992

Serres M, 1968 *Hermès I - La communication* (Minuit, Paris)

Serres M, 1977 *Hermès IV. La distribution* (Minuit, Paris)

Severino E, 1979 *Legge e caso* (Adelphi, Milano)

Severino E, 1980, *Destino della necessità* (Adelphi, Milano)

Sica P, 1981 *Storia dell'urbanistica. Il Settecento* (Laterza, Roma-Bari)

Simmel G, 1908 *Soziologie. Untersuchungen über die Formen der Vergesellschaftung* (Duncker & Humblot, Berlin)

Weber M, 1956 *Wirtschaft und Gesellschaft*, 4th ed., Ed J Winckelmann (Mohr-Siebeck, Tübingen). English translation: University of California Press, Berkeley 1978

Weyl H, 1949 *Philosophy of Mathematics and Natural Science* (Princeton University Press, Princeton)

FINITE SPECIFICITY

by Ulf Strohmayer and Matthew Hannah

'If you look to your left, you will see a typical family of peasants, tending the soil as their ancestors have done for generations,' the tour guide said, intruding on my enjoyment of the bright orange birds off to the right. Reluctantly, I turned, and found the 'peasant family' anything but typical. They were truly ugly, which both fascinated and repelled me. I recalled the wisdom of the native clerk at the duty-free shop: 'You can't judge a melon by its skin.' I wonder what that family would have thought about the native clerk. Especially if he had appeared in those clothes.

* * *

The terrain of the social sciences has been relandscaped once again. We are no longer shaded by the great trees of Truth, having opted instead to cultivate knowledge in the Bonsai tradition. Will it be possible in this way to sustain our shady interests, our interests in defensible knowledge? In geography as elsewhere, the death of simple causality has engendered a 'shrinkage' in the scale at which knowledge is expected and sought. Geographers in particular have turned this growing theoretical modesty into a source of renewed legitimacy. No longer simply a fly in the scientific soup, the specificity of places is now presented as a principled and necessary qualification of any social understanding. Theory (nomothetic 'formula') and description (ideographic 'catalogue') have been collapsed into one another, producing (it is hoped) an understanding of uniqueness 'in and of itself,' and simultaneously 'as a window on society at large.' The rigid and barren distinction between 'general' and 'particular' has been abandoned upon the 'discovery' that the two are mutually constitutive. Hence the recent popularity of realism, 'structuration theory,' and the various versions of 'local history' within geography. Whereas 'grand theory' shaded the researcher from the need to choose amongst different explanatory concepts, the new practice calls for an increased sensitivity in deploying categories. 'Determination in the last instance,' economic or otherwise, is replaced by a multiplicity of determinations *in this* instance, by specificity as an ongoing process-in-place.

* * *

But does it work? Although the guises of 'specificity' are many ('uniqueness of place,' 'local knowledge,' 'particularity,' 'locale'), in each instance it presents a paradox as a workable synthesis, a condition of unrelatability as the basis for a meaningful relation. In other words, every possible instantiation of 'specificity' would have to be both unrelatable to other instantiations and recognizable *as* another instantiation. But recognizing two instantiations (whether in the form of 'processes,' or 'structurated situations') is a way of relating them. So 'the specific' always incorporates a wound or a rupture between the *condition* of its intelligibility and its intelligibility. 'Authentic' specificity could never be named and every named 'specificity' is 'inauthentic.' Which is to say that 'specificity' *as we can know it* is but another way of disguising an a priori generality. If knowledge is to be sought in 'the specific,' it remains unattainable. Like any idea of truth, or even 'plausibility,'[1] 'specificity' requires a hollowness that renders its 'aboutness' simultaneously possible and futile.

* * *

We can read the turn to specificity as the logical conclusion of attempts to bypass the tension between 'formula' and 'catalogue' through a reduction in scale. The failure (or 'deconstruction') of this strategy reveals the invocation of any 'critical distance' as little more than a re-upholstering, in positive and 'politically correct' colours, of the inescapable hollowness, the emptiness within the hermeneutic

---

[1] Does 'plausibility' suffice where 'truth' has been discredited as a yardstick for knowledge? We think not. Judgements of plausibility like judgements of truth, depend on the very same paradoxical im-/possibility of relating an 'explanation' to 'that which it is supposed to explain.' If such a connection were not assumed possible, the assertion that any single explanation is 'more' or 'less' plausible than any other would be unintelligible. In other words, the failings of 'truth' are also fatal to plausibility.

circle. Whereas theoretical practices so far have been considered 'responsible' in proportion to their commitment to solving this problem, a more radical notion of responsibility would begin with the admission that the problem is insoluble, that these hollow spaces cannot be eliminated. The concern of this less forgiving responsibility would be *what to do* with the categorial vacuum.

* * *

It would seem that these spaces are inevitable. But since we understand why they are, we should be able to overcome the obstacle to knowledge that they initially posed. The interpretation of a paradox, like that of anything else, makes it intelligible on a different level, thereby allowing it to function discursively in the manner of a new bone growth around a fracture.

Or so we lead ourselves to believe. But any new 'bone growth' is always already ruptured (i.e. 'deconstructable'), thereby rendering the functionality of any meta-interpretation of paradoxes a lie.

But is not the presence of interpretation better than its absence? Surely, though we may never be able to recognize knowledge as such, it is still more likely to be hiding somewhere in the attempt to communicate than in silence.

A question doomed always to be hypothetical since neither choice, as a choice *in principle,* excuses us from continued participation in the world of language. Despite the deconstructability of all knowledge, *again in principle*, nihilism can only ever

117

be a straw figure. Like it or not, we must deposit language, deconstructive or otherwise, as we stumble along.

* * *

Behind us we leave *monuments*. Some of them we inevitably read as *documents*, as 'facts', 'interpretations,' 'evidence,' in short, as carriers of meaning. Deconstruct*able* as any claim of documentarity is, only a limited number of deconstructions are ever pursued; deconstructability must be *made* relevant. Which is to say that the mute existence of language does not depend on the argumentative defense of the assumption that it means. While the deconstruction of one 'document' does not immediately affect others *per se*, their respective deconstruct*abilities* might. We say 'might,' because the space between deconstructability and actual deconstruction matters: the latter only proceeds in a finite fashion and will always be exceeded by the infinite possibilities of the former.

* * *

Finitude thus emerges as the condition of possibility of meaning.

What a strange 'thus'...

Think about it: the impossibility of deconstructing everything is simultaneously the necessity to assume some meaning. Contrary to our normal modes of justification, intelligibility depends not on a surplus of answers, but instead on a deficit of questions. Turning to wield a question leaves unquestioned meaning 'behind one's back.' We find meaning where we ignore, or never initially suspect, that we cannot.

Why should we find the meaning of 'meaning' in the neglect of deconstruct-ability? Why should the consideration of finitude dictate our understanding of meaning?

'Finitude' does not 'dictate' anything. It is simply a recognition of the imperative of choices, including the decision whether or not to interpret meaning as optional. In other words, the necessity for bracketing *can* be bracketed. Documentarity is only possible on the basis of the monumental occurrence of language, a basis it would have to efface in order to survive. That which makes the document possible confiscates its legitimacy.

* * *

The makeshift legitimacy of the social sciences is thus 'based' on a two-layered disguise. First, the de-legitimizing effect of the occurrence of language, its 'monumental' character, is covered over. And second, even the supposed legitimacy jeopardized by the muteness of occurrence is itself rendered questionable once it is viewed as an outgrowth of the failure to question.

* * *

And yet, is not the recognition of 'finitude' as the condition of im-/possibility of meaning itself only possible after passing through the assumption of meaning? Does not this temporal precondition render the seeming priority of the monument derivative? The thrownness into 'history,' in other words, always predates its retrospective interpretation as a neglect of deconstructability, and hence also the excavation of this neglect.

A temporal priority, on the other hand, is still the occurrence of one meaning ('belief') before another meaning ('suspension of belief'). For the second to occur as 'conditioned' by the first, both still have to occur. While in a temporal sense documentarity precedes the idea of monumentality, it can only do so as an occurrence. The 'intelligibility' of 'thrownness' hinges in turn on the thrownness of intelligibility.

* * *

And *vice versa ad infinitum.* 'Conditions of possibility,' assumed to act in concert with one another, are traditionally assigned the task of limiting 'relativism,' 'irrationalism,' 'nihilism,' 'fictionality,' etc. By stabilizing the juxtaposition of monument and document into a specific polar geometry, they allow for an indestructible *Ur*-meaning. But this stability *can* only be assumed upon the decision to ignore the incommensurability and mutual antagonism between temporal and a-temporal 'conditions of possibility.' Even the deconstruction of any such geometry would have to establish a 'control in exile' through such terms as 'incommen-surability,' *'différance,'* or 'monument.' Only when 'conditions of possibility' are forcibly recognized as acting in harmony, can we meaningfully speak of 'monuments,' 'documents,' or any hybrid of the two. 'Conditions of possibility' *are not* in any unified, meaningful sense, and it is only finitude, i.e. the limited ability to question, that allows us to assume meaning in the face of their invocation, or to invoke 'conditions of possibility' in the face of their aggregate meaninglessness.

* * *

Reinvigorated as the hinge of *this* discussion, 'specificity' would appear at the point where the chaotic confluence of temporal and a-temporal 'conditions of possibility' is domesticated. Constructed as an intelligible point of contact between mute 'finitude' and talkative 'thrownness,' or between 'monumentality' and 'documentarity,' 'specificity' thus once again builds meaning on meaninglessness. Its utterance is the event that forces together the incompatible and disguises this coercion as obedience to necessity. But the directionless cacophony of 'conditions of possibility' necessitates neither 'specificity' nor any other artificial *détente*. In fact, this noise constantly militates against any such shotgun wedding.

* * *

The space between mutually exclusive 'conditions of possibility' is the space of the event. Mute and talkative at the same time, any event must be either trusted or mistrusted, without recourse to a standard of 'vigilance.' The assumption of meaning or meaninglessness is only arbitrarily prejudiced, but prejudiced it will always be. No 'ontology,' or bracketing of the abyss of 'ontology,' can ever be basic. This impasse can inspire awe or disgust, indifference or commitment, without any particular response being necessarily more 'intellectually honest' than any other. Similarly, 'political' responsibility, regardless of the commitment by which it is motivated, comes as an event and is thus naked and disarmed while not therefore ineffective. The determination and autonomy which we all simultaneously embody ultimately teach us nothing about each other, our 'selves,' or what we should do.

* * *

This being said, it remains for us to recognize that we have accomplished nothing. Having written a document that neither answers any questions nor prescribes any direction, we still find ourselves compelled to critically interact with events, texts, and, yes, 'history.' As we rejoice in the trappings of a Pennsylvania spring, Matt is busy forcing together Foucault, Althusser and the plight of the Lakota, while Ulf is still caught up in an effort to understand Heidegger's entanglement in '1933.' Writing after ontology might not answer any of our pertinent questions, but then writing under the sign of ontology produces answers only by avoiding these questions. Commitments and idiosyncrasies should be dry-cleaned periodically. Or not.

References

Althusser L, 1979 *For Marx* trans. B Brewester (Verso, London)

Deleuze G, 1988 *Foucault* trans. S Hand (University of Minnesota Press, Minneapolis)

Derrida J, 1982 *Of Grammatology* trans. G Spivak (The Johns Hopkins Press, Baltimore)

Foucault M, 1972 *The Archeology of Knowledge* trans. A M.Sheridan Smith (Pantheon, New York)

Heidegger M, 1962 *Being and Time* trans. J Macquarrie, E Robinson (Harper & Row, New York)

Heidegger M, 1971 *On the Way to Language* trans. P D Hertz (Harper & Row, New York)

Lacoue-Labarthe P, 1990 *Heidegger, Art and Politics* trans. C Turner (Basil Blackwell, Cambridge, Ma.)

Nancy J-L, 1990 *Une pensée finie* (Galilée, Paris)

Wittgenstein L, 1953 *Philosophical Investigations* trans. G E M Anscombe (MacMillan, New York)

SPACES OF MISREPRESENTATION

by Peter Gould

Music makers and dreamers

The theme "Limits to Representation" is no longer problematic. It was dissolved long ago. We are the re-presenters, presenting again that which comes to presence in us. Like many poets, the Irishman O'Shaughnessy knew this in his bones:

*We are the music makers,
And we are the dreamers of dreams.*[1]

And we are the re-presenters, the projectors, the positors, and in our humanity have no choice. It requires that we are with others. If a private language made no sense to Wittgenstein, a private, with-no-other "world" makes no sense either. "Sense" requires others: the wholly private world is the knived-off world of the autistic, of the schizophrenic. Or so I must suppose. I have never been there. Even the intensely private drive to self-fulfillment, an endeavor filled with moments of reverie and quiet reflection, still takes place in a world with others. I find myself always in a "world" and in a world shared with others. The former shapes, gives meaning, to the latter. In a carefully qualified and delimited sense, too ponderous to outline here,[2] I am that "world", for to claim humanness, rather than simple

---

[1] Arthur O'Shaughnessy, The Music Makers, *a much anthologized poem, deservedly so, I feel, for its beauty, for its rhythm, and for the various levels at which it may be read.*

[2] *And anyway I could not approach the succinctness or insight of Richard Rorty's highly professional Introduction to his* Objectivity, Relativism, and Truth: Philosophical Papers, Vol. I *(1991a, pp.1-17). There he expresses the wish "that English-speaking philosophy of the twenty-first century will have put the representationalist problematic behind it, as most French- or German-speaking philosophy already has" (p.12). Yet even in his Deweyan world of "a community which strives after both intersubjective agreement and novelty" (p.13), marked by a Davidsonian "account of how marks and noises made by certain organisms hang together in a coherent pattern" (p.10), taking off from Darwin as "beliefs as adaptations to the environment rather than quasi-pictures" (p.10), a starting point for which*

physiomorphological similarity, I can be no other.

The particular "world" that I have become is questionable in itself. It contains the condition of possibility for questioning, for speculating, for sharing re-presenting in its most distinctive condition of possibility, language itself. We re-present in language. Now that the problematic has been dissolved, how difficult it is to catch the problematic. How could a word ever have been thought to be the thing itself? The signified, the signifier?

It is quite understandable why, before the dissolving, we paid, and are still paying, so much attention to language. Again, in a carefully delimited sense, it is us; and in large part our world comes to us, we come to ourselves, in language. Awareness, intense awareness of language, is an awareness of ourselves. Perhaps to "Know Thyself" is to know one's self in language, to attempt an awareness of self in language akin to Heidegger's driving insistence that we recapture and renew the most elemental force of words. As words slip into common parlance and become taken-for-granted, loosing their bite and first fresh shock of illumination and seeing, so we slip into "das Man". Inevitably we slip back. We all have everyday lives to lead, where, it seems to me, thoroughly pragmatic considerations shape much of what we do. We have to get on with things, we need things that work. No one can sustain the high notes of Thinking for long.[3] Some never try. Others become enraptured by a sudden fresh mo-

"there is simply no way to give sense to the idea of ... our language as systematically out of phase with what lies beyond our skins" (p.12), still, and as I note in the text below, as human beings, rather than pandas and narwhals, things come to presence in us as meaning, and these meanings are shared with others. We re-present to others that which has come to presence, usually in language, but sometimes in other ways known to children, physicists and lovers. This sense of re-presenting, or so it seems to me, is a condition of possibility of being human, and is etymologically embedded in "communication." It says nothing, and does not require us to ask anything, about the infinite regress of conditions of conditions of ... possibility. Those who re-present may stand in awe at Being as the condition of possibility of all human "worlds," or the totally inexplicable is of isness, but this clearly does not come easily to pragmatists. So far as I can see, they find absolutely nothing awful, and on this final point I must still cling to my childlike ways, and wave goodbye to Richard Rorty with a rather puzzled look on my face.

3 I capitalize Thinking only to emphasize Heidegger's special meaning of the term, a meaning explicated in many places, but especially in Martin Heidegger's essay Science and Reflection, in The Question Concerning Technology and Other Essays *(1977)*.

ment of seeing, and in their clinging to it drag it down from the realm of the Thinker to the level of the Scribbler. We all do it. In the rough seas of Thinking we all gasp for breath, we all grasp a lifebuoy floating by stenciled with "The Good Ship Marx" ... "Saussure"... "Heidegger"... "Derrida"... and other frail vessels who have left their lifesaving flotsam behind after their own finite journeys. After that first moment of elation, of finding new buoyancy, we forget that even lifebuoys, when submerged too long, become waterlogged. And yet we still cling ... and forget how to swim.

Does it make a difference?

In our concern for ourselves as language, in our attempts to be aware of the elemental force of language, does it make a difference? Do we think, do we write, *differently*? Does it show to others? Does it matter if it shows to others? Show, not in the pretentiousness of striving to show *off*, but show in the quiet awareness of contingency, the stillness of humility, the gentle wryness of knowing impermanency, in the occasional flash of disclosing. In our awareness of self in language, have we raised another pseudoproblem? Does our awareness "(turn) upon a difference which 'makes no difference'"?[4] Does the awareness of humble contingency and impermanency inform, make more penetrating, the disclosing?

We are driving language, we are driving ourselves, hard. Thinking about language in language, about ourselves to ourselves, demands hard and anxious driving. It is not an easy task. So why do we do it? What drives us? Why bother? Why try to re-present a re-presentation? Why try to construct it? Why try to deconstruct it? As an end in itself? As a means to an end? What end? Who cares? Does it make a difference? As a moment of language's intense awareness of itself in language ... what happens? Or is this sentence non-sense, a

---

4 *Richard Rorty (1991b, p.17), quoting William James. In proper acknowledgement, I shall try to reference each borrowing from this series of provocative essays, but anyone who has read them will recognize my greater debt to a catalyst for whatever thinking (definitely lower case) that is here.*

meaning not shared, a *munus*, a present, that is not *co(m)*, with, anything, not shared, not com-municated? Just another pseudoproblem of the reification of language to something other than ourselves? But whether reified to something other by us, or acknowledged to be a condition of possibility of ourselves, does such an intensified awareness matter? Does it change anything? The way we think? The way we write? The matters we choose to write about? Or whether we choose to write at all, anymore?

Three "weak thoughts"

Because I have read too much, and thought too little, because this is what some Italian philosophers call "weak thought",[5] I can see only three choices, possibilities, ways out of this cracked fly bottle flung upon the beach. The first is to set one's feet firmly on the path of the *avant-garde*, to be at the mocking, and often self-mocking edge for its own sake. Perhaps even with an awareness that one is caught up in the production-line-to-redundancy way of commenting about the world, an entrapment so common to much "postmodern" geographic writing that it is, ironically, a post-Fordist way of writing on the edge of redundancy and planned obsolescence. Perhaps it is with an awareness that a *telos* has appeared once again, and just as we thought we had got rid of it. Perhaps it is a choice made even while acknowledging that deconstruction itself is a templating, a particular framework, a particular *way* chosen to be in the world of texts, and, therefore, despite all the shrill denials, a method, one of those abhorred methods, nevertheless. It is, to scramble the metaphor thoroughly, the white toga approach, sitting in the margined seats of the colosseum called Discourse, raising or lowering one's thumb in properly modulated, yet still gleeful, disdain at the efforts of those down there in the textual arena. Ribald suggestions of cowardness, calls from the arena to join in the fray, are met with a properly cynical condescension only the truly vulgar deserve. After all, the last vestiges of blood and sand might never wash off, and, anyway, the

---

5 *Gianni Vattimo and Pier Aldo Rovatti (1983), quoted by Rorty (1991b, p.6).*

cleaning bill for one's togas would be quite unbearable.

The second choice is a move to such intense awareness that we are driven to mute linguistic impotence. Perhaps we have hints of the possibility of such moves in the passing over to silence of Wittgenstein, in the *Gelassenheit*, the releasement, of Heidegger, when he says "a regard for metaphysics still prevails even in the intention to overcome metaphysics. Therefore our task is to cease all overcoming, and leave metaphysics to itself."[6] Perhaps, who knows, the madness of a Nietzsche ended in a similar silence? Here the intensity of our awareness of being language paralyzes us, mocks us into some sort of higher form of "writer's block." We become so self-depreciatingly aware that we have no choice but to remain silent. But if language is us, a condition of possibility of being human, then mute silence, induced by too-intense awareness, takes away, or smothers, our humanity, takes us out of a larger shared world of re-presentation; first, to the cloister of esotericism, and from that still-shared cloister to the cell, the private prison, of solitude. I fear this in its many manifestations. From my world I see some, who could have given much, in permanent retreat. I fear it because I do not know how to call them out into the sunlight again, to meet with me in the *agora*, that bustling, colorful marketplace of ideas. And in the darkness too many die by their own hand.[7] Too many poets kill themselves. And I think we should ask why.

"Then", he said brightly, "there is a third way." This is to eschew the coteries of esoteric cloisters, to dismiss the dark and impotent silences of lonely cells, and enter the sunlit *agora* again. It is to strip off the white toga of deconstructive disdain, and enter the arena once again – or even for the first time. It is to join with others in the human task of illuminating the marvellous "worlds" in which we find ourselves thrown. "But that means," say the silent prisoners and languid thumb pointers, "that means we shall find ourselves among

---

6 Martin Heidegger (1972, p.24), quoted by Rorty (1991b, p.95).

7 Concretely, this has private meaning in the self-destruction of a loved and much respected friend, who happened to be an historian, rather than a poet. But I do not think this is a unique experience by any means. Many know, quite tragically, how to fill in this blank with other names.

the vulgar once again, and who will be there to tell us apart from the mob?" But if the acknowledgement of silence and the awareness of the deconstructed margin *mean* anything, then the acknowledged awareness will make a difference, and a difference requires no telling apart. By their *words* ye shall know them. At least, if they dare to accept a challenge to put up or shut up that is more than a hoisting of a thumb, or a closing to mute incoherence.

Representation and misrepresentation

The problematic of re-presentation has been dissolved, and so too has the problematic of its limits. Its limits are us; they can be nowhere else. But does this imply that the theme "Limits to Representation" is banal, leading once again, with weary repetitiveness, to mocking disdain or unshared silence? Not at all. For if the problematic has been dissolved, we are still left, as human beings and geographers, with the manner in which we shall re-present, and so share a present, an illumination granted to us in all the finite contingency of its historical moment. And in this condition of possibility lies, of course, the possibility of mis-representation. The possibility of a true representation as opposed to a false one. As humans we cannot avoid truth and falsity. *Pace* Derrida, and the rest of the updated pantheon, there are not *just* texts: there are texts that bring out of concealment, and there are texts that deliberately or mistakenly, but always falsely, try to conceal, to take something from the light into darkness, or to keep something seen hidden from others.[8] What is problematic is not representation or misrepresentation, but how these play themselves out in the everyday worlds of people. And for us, how they play out in the worlds of the geographer, perhaps especially the geographer in the academy and the university.

---

8 One cannot help a certain wry and chuckling laugh when the Derridas of this world are hoisted by a petard lit by a Rorty. He notes Derrida's indignation at having his own text "deconstructed" after the manner in which he indulges his own per chance for unraveling. As a result, his metaphysical claims are seen to lie starkly within the same tradition as that from which he is trying to extricate himself. He does not like this unconcealing one bit (Rorty, 1991b, pp.101-102).

So I shall now try to practice what I preach. If nothing else, my text may serve as a source of employment for those who take the path of deconstruction. After all, "You can't have ... a margin without a page of text."[9] And, anyway, most of them are good fellows, and have to earn their bread in the ways they know best.

The palace of misrepresentation

The Academy, in its daily life of pragmatic, ideologically-informed governance, and in its intellectual life of learning and teaching, is a vast space, a glittering palace, for misrepresentation. Claiming reason, truth, justice, resolution by polite and attentive discourse, it contradicts its assertions at every turn by gross unfairness, dissimulating lies, strident and angry shouting, and irrational behavior so comic that the angels weep only tears of celestial laughter. To devote one's life to this human comedy, and even bend one's best efforts to sustain it, one has to be totally without humor (generally, but not exclusively, the academic administration), or tinged with madness (generally, but not exclusively, the faculty). It has been my home for nearly forty years, and I love it dearly. Most comic of all, I even get paid for what I do.[10]

The field of misrepresentations arising from contradictions is so large, and contains such splendid examples, that one can only pick out a few, highly diverse, and too often tabooed topics. I write the word "tabooed" with great care and awareness, not only because it has the splendid and slightly naughty "ooo" sound of Ooolsson to it, redolent of mysterious anthropological disclosure, but because it invokes the shadow of "political correctness" that sends a chill down the necks of old-fashioned Enlightenment inheritors like me.[11]

9 *Rorty, 1991b, p.94*
10 *Too much by far, according to some reviewers of the National Science Foundation, who quickly turned to the budget page, and thought it appropriate to make this comment as part of the scientific evaluation of a proposal. How pure and scientifically objective can we get?*
11 *Yes I know, the Enlightenment's ideals are subject to nihilistic deconstruction along with everything else. I think I know most, or at least many, of the arguments against such a set of pathetically naive and irrational beliefs. Yet they remain informative of my "world," particularly my view of what the university ought to be.*

Political correctness has been around as long as there have been universities. We are always, and usually quite properly, getting into trouble; which is why, for truly democratic societies, universities are so terribly important. But usually the danger is from without, the wolf-like Assyrian is battering on Babylon's gates. Today, the matter of political correctness is more insidious, it is internal, the belly of the horse has discharged its warriors, and the danger is within. Not that the inside and outside can always be clearly distinguished today; the intellectual walls of the Ivory Tower are highly permeable, and physically the open campus is a mark of most, especially state, universities in America.[12] But in the daily life of governance, let me point to two misrepresentations arising from contradiction.[13]

Conforming to diversity

The first is the issue of diversity, an issue that most fairminded people welcome as a topic of concerned discourse. As a further genuine attempt to open up greater opportunity for self-fulfillment, no thoughtful member of a democratic society could find persuasive

---

12 *I have in my possession an extraordinary document, written by a poet who served as a temporary president of Skidmore College, at a time when it was planning to move from old, and inadequate quarters to a new campus. Because of a sudden death, and the hiatus that followed, no directions had been given by the Board of Trustees to the architects. When this became apparent, the poet left the room, secluded herself for half an hour, and set down firm directions to realize her own extraordinary vision of what a small undergraduate university should be. One of its distinguishing marks was that it should have no walls, but that it should have one, secluded place to build a small ivory tower.*

13 *Let me make it quite clear that these are general problems facing many American universities, perhaps especially, but by no means exclusively, state universities. Almost anyone teaching in an American university today can relate similar problems, so I am not in any sense choosing these examples from my own university exclusively. It certainly has some of these problems, but probably to a lesser degree than many others. In certain respects my own university may be more alert to some of these difficulties than most, although often in a state of indecision and equivocation about how to deal with them in a fair and acceptable way. The choices are often not obvious, especially in light of tremendous pressures external to it, general requirements and enforcements that particular circumstances may make it difficult, if not impossible, to meet immediately.*

arguments to oppose it.*14* Yet the issue is rapidly being pushed to its own contradiction, and diversity now requires increasingly such uniformitarianism of opinion that it is rapidly approaching the sort of despotism to which writers such as Tocqueville, Mill and Orwell pointed (Berlin, 1991, p.45). How ironic that "diversity" requires the elimination of diverse opinion about it, particularly when we know that any "solution" is always going to create its own contradictions, throwing up new conditions breeding new examples of age old problems (Berlin, 1991, p.14). Why, when we know this (and those whose views are informed by Marxism, if they have done their Hegelian homework, should know this better than most), why when we know this are we not alert to it? Why do we fail to acknowledge such an apparent inevitability?

For in the wake of the current drive to diversity comes misrepresentation and injustice, neither of which should be tolerated, let alone promoted, by a university. Scholarships, for example, are given solely on the basis of the melanin content of one's skin, or whether one can trace a name to the Iberian peninsula, no matter how remote such ties are, or what the present socio-economic status or need might be. This is patently discriminatory and unjust. Other descendants of Europeans, whose origins were north and east of the Pyrenees – the Olssons, Strohmayers, Farinellis, ... – are effectively eliminated by "the allocation of always scarce resources." So are all the other descendants of those who contributed, and are still contributing, to the American melting pot. "But," say the diversifiers, "there is a long legacy of discrimination to put right here, and it may require drastic measures." To which I reply: "By visiting the sins of the great great grandparents on their great great grandchildren? Are we still so Judaic and biblical as to invoke the Book of Joel (1:3)? Do we never forget and start again? Does the feud never end? Do I, as a former off-shore barbarian, still claim reparations

---

14 Like Rorty, and for virtually the same reasons (Rorty, 1991b, pp.135-139), I welcome the opening up of more possibilities to achieve awareness and self-fulfillment in a democratic society. I am not quite as sanguine as he is that a balance will be maintained that easily. And "balance," in my use, is not the same as the "equilibrium" of a status quo.

from Italians for their imperialistic act of colonization.[15] Or I do stop after receiving Norwegian compensation for the acts of rape, pillage and murder "we" had to endure at "their" hands?

It will not do: justice is not retrieved by injustice. And truth should be sayable, in the open, not taken into concealment. State governors may wish, or be forced, to rewrite the history and geography of New York in light of what is currently "politically correct," but they should be reminded that such rewritings have tended to be the marks of despots not democrats.[16] At the moment that Zora Hurston's novel, *Their Eyes Were Watching God*, is retrieved and brought into the light (Rorty, 1991b, p.138), will the works of Twain and Conrad go into concealment?[17] For increasingly the mark of political correctness is becoming the touchstone of sayability. In recognizing the sheer power of such censorship, one is increasingly *en garde*, defensive, holding one's tongue, remaining silent.

Let me give a concrete example of how, today, the truth is not "politically correct." We have reached the point in the university where it would be unthinkable to declare in public that Martin Luther King was a "hypocritical fornicating priest." We are in a world today where afternoon seminars are cancelled by a university administration in order to "persuade" students to attend an address by some unknown politician on the occasion of King's birthday. It seems legitimate to argue that the work of learning and teaching are much more important than this gesture of political correctness. If a university administration can roll the birthdays of Washington (The

---

15 *In light of our greater sensitivity, it is quite clear that a number of descriptions of my ancestors by Roman writers should be excised from existing texts, and certainly should not be assigned as part of a school or university curriculum, within which there are always impressionable, even corruptible youth.*

16 *Governor Cuomo has decreed the elimination of all "offensive" place names from the maps of New York State. One wonders how this issue arose, or how it was accomplished. Was there a Politically Acceptable Place Names Committee appointed, whose members scanned lists and maps, recommending the excision of names whose historical import might have been useful, in pedagogic circumstances, for sensitizing people to the unthought assumptions of earlier "worlds"? What will happen to poor old Intercourse, Pennsylvania, when the prurient-minded set up a similar committee?*

17 *How will the language of Twain's* Huckleberry Finn *be sanitized? Or a title like* The Nigger of the Narcissus *appear in future courses?*

Father of His Country) and Lincoln (The Great Emancipator) into one "President's Day," and then consign it to public oblivion, it exhibits unwarranted authoritarianism by cancelling major functions of the university for a lesser figure. Now if I had declared that phrase in public (as I am doing here), I would have been condemned outright as totally insensitive at best, and downright racist at worst. The latter symptomatic of the fact that it is difficult, to the point of virtual impossibility, for a white person to criticize anyone of color, or a male to criticize a female, in the university today. The opposite brings no such penalties, and, indeed, often finds an encouraging and sympathetic hearing.

Yet this descriptive phrase, by all trustworthy accounts of those close to King, is perfectly true. Notice I have nothing against fornication *per se*; it seems to me a personal matter of private choice. John and Robert Kennedy, both of whom I admire greatly, a legacy of earlier but still-enduring bourgeois liberal days, were apparently gluttons for it, and by all accounts considerably adept at it. My admiration is not diminished one wit by their private sexual peccadillos.[18] But they did not climb into the high pulpit each Sunday, preach against it, and then practice it assiduously the other six days of the week. That, it strikes me, is a pretty good example of high hypocrisy, something I dislike in students and fellow faculty – and in myself, when I can detect it, which I quite frequently do. I suppose it has something to do with Caesar's wife: if you teach a course on ethics, and urge ethical conduct on others, should you not practice what you preach? So it is quite truthful to describe King as a

---

18 Nor is my admiration diminished in the slightest for King's physical courage, although I remain highly skeptical in general about the efficacy of non-violent protests, unless they take place within a still more or less democratic society. I do not think Ghandi and his followers would have stood a ghost of a chance in Hitler's Germany, Pol Pot's Cambodia, Stalin's Soviet Union, or Idi Amin's Uganda. They would have been quickly eliminated, and no one would have heard of them, let alone remembered them later. But I admire and am grateful to those who protest nonviolently in my own, and other reasonably democratic societies, since they are often effective in making these societies live up to their declared, even constitutionally declared, ideals. I suppose, when it comes down to it, that I am opposed to the elevation of human beings to gods by the vulgar process of mythologization. Human beings are not perfectible, and I think King, as a Christian minister, would have been the first to agree. At least I hope so, even while recalling that all power corrupts.

"hypocritical, fornicating priest" – he was certainly all of these – yet shockingly and politically unacceptable to do so. Notice it was just as shockingly and politically incorrect to describe Adolph Hitler truthfully in the 1930s, so unacceptable that you probably would have lost your life. From all perspectives, left and right, telling the truth about mythologized heros is simply not ... politically correct.

Tenure and the freedom to be

The second, and I think important area of misrepresentation and contradiction comes in the intensely formalized and bureaucratized process of granting promotion and tenure. It was a formalization driven, as most human constructs are, by a mixture of motives. The first was to ensure justice; the second, too often not mentioned, was fear and embarrassment of legal suit. But then legal suits generally arise when injustice is felt, so the question of avoiding embarrassment could be nicely concealed in the public stance of righteous morality. The formalization seems to have begun about 10 or 15 years ago, after the heydays of dissent and campus upheavals in the late Sixties. Young faculty who supported such dissent, or who engaged in such nefarious projects as faculty unionization, were later found to be lacking in the expected attributes of teaching, research and scholarship, and were invited to seek careers elsewhere.[19] It took only a few legal confrontations, combined with a much more strident voice of feminism, to put into place more open procedures in which the judges (for so they are), are made to be more personally responsible by their somewhat more public accountability. This

---

19 Many of us have written strong letters of protest over the past 10 or 15 years when such injustices came to our attention, and, like Amnesty International, have succeeded in shining such an embarrassing light on some cases that the decisions were reversed. But we also know of egregious cases of injustice, often, but by no means exclusively, to women, which were extremely difficult to fight because of the concealed, and therefore dark, nature of the decision process. As for "leftist" activities, such as promulgating the advantages of unionization (to which I personally, and in my particular circumstances, opposed, though certainly not in principle), I know of cases where administrative power was misused to punish, though I could not bring a shred of evidence to bear in a court of law. One is left with the sort of numb and frustrating lump one always feels in the face of an injustice that one has no power to put right.

is all to the good, even if the process has become much more time-consuming and bureaucratically ponderous.[20]

Yet I cannot help feeling (some would say in my aged white male way), a sense of nostalgia for the old days. I cannot recall 20 and 30 years ago the issues of promotion and tenure ever arising with the anxiety-creating force that they do today, and I do not think my lack of recalling is unique or too far off base. There were certain, but certainly unformalized and unwritten, sets of expectations: good teaching; good, that is to say respected, learning, and publishing what you had learnt; helping students in all sorts of ways, but especially those requiring those sounding board activities called academic guidance; and then taking one's share of the burdens of those thoroughly tiresome, but somebody's-got-to-do-it, bits and pieces of administration. All of these once taken-for-granted expectations are now highly formalized in a set of written and published decrees.[21] In the days recalled by nostalgia, promotion and tenure came along a roughly expected intervals if one had "kept one's end up." You heard of someone pushing for promotion, usually in the context of invitations to explore other possibilities, but it was a dangerous game to play if you liked being where you were, and enjoyed what you were doing. Someone might urge you to make a choice you did not want to make.

Nostalgia or not, and while still acknowledging the possible opportunities for injustice, both of commission and omission, I cannot

---

20 *This will seem very strange to Scandinavians, for whom the award of a professorial chair is usually achieved by a process of totally public evaluation. Published evidence from candidates is read by members of an evaluating committee, who then write lengthy, and always public, evaluations, supporting their view that X is preferable to Y. Like any human system it is not perfect, making mistakes of omission and commission, and being subject to a certain amount of manipulation. But with a harsh, and hardly disinterested, public light glaring on the process, it is perhaps more difficult for rampant injustices to be perpetrated.*

21 *The process seems to be an almost perfect counterexample of Rorty's gloss on Putnam, when he notes the civilizing move "to substitute* phronesis *for codification," while viewing codification as an example "of the positivistic idea that rationality is a matter of applying criteria" (Rorty, 1991a, p.25), an idea to be distrusted. Especially distrusted, I would say, in the evaluation of human beings, because, and as I note below, there are few things more capable of producing contradiction and injustice than criteria perverted by well-intentioned positivists who must reify other human beings. It is uncomfortable to recall Heidegger's caution, "We are all positivists today."*

recall that much anxiety on anyone's part. Almost invariably a person knew, and his or her colleagues knew, whether that person would fit into a particular department, college and university. Including the awkward sons (and increasingly daughters)-of-bitches, with all sorts of rough edges, who you had to admit nevertheless were damned good teachers, fine and insightful scholars, fantastically well-organized and supportive and fair administrators, or sometimes, miraculously, all three.

All this has changed. I am distressed at the high levels of anxiety often displayed now by young faculty, and I am frankly shocked by the obscenity of some of the procedures I hear being imposed on them elsewhere. I say "obscenity," because the very procedures set up and put into place to represent a just and fair process of judgement have now been turned into authoritarian impositions that misrepresent the spirit of free inquiry and individual responsibility that should be at the heart of any university worthy of the name. Promotion and tenure recommendations are now supported by dossiers well over an inch thick, subdivided into color-coded sections recording the meritorious performances in each carefully defined category. Young faculty members certainly know *where* they are, but they possess little freedom to be *what* they are.

One hears increasingly of young, untenured faculty being assigned what are ostensibly mentoring, but in fact monitoring, committees. Made up of suitably aged and professionally obsequious "tribal elders," they regularly review the waxing *curriculum vitae* and point out that publications in refereed journals are what really counts, and even assign points to various journals considered by the elder statespersons to be more prestigious than others. Providing high point publications anchor a cv, a modest dallying in journals "outside" the field is permitted, even mildly encouraged, but not too much, of course. After all, it is not really geography. Or sociology, or economics, or any one of the intellectually defensive, and therefore perniciously arrogant fields that purvey their wares under the respectable, but oxymoronic title of the social *sciences.*

What is worse, there seem to be young faculty around who like it this way, as a prisoner will appreciate the well-ordered routine and well-established expectations of his prison life. After all, you *do* know where you are. Once upon a time, there was a clear distinction between a university, an army brigade, a branch of a large corporation, and a Washington bureaucracy. Many, especially those who have served in the latter, have a hard time telling them apart, bringing to the university an authoritarianism destructive of that precious and irreplaceable morale that comes from free and responsible inquiry. It is an insidious downward process: one even hears of young faculty conveying, almost to the point of imposition, their own anxious expectations on new graduate students ("After all, you'll get your name on the paper at the annual meeting"), when the graduate students may have had little or no experience of research, are unsure of exactly where they want to go, or whether they have any real interest in the topic assigned. From tenured tribal elder monitoring the angst-laden new doctorate, to the new PhD inculcating the tribal mores to the candidate for the next *rite-de-passage*, there is the unspoken assumption that you will achieve the highest reaches of human endeavor when *you* become like *me*.

All this has nothing to do with human freedom or self-fulfillment. It has much to do with a sort of self-imposed slavery, substituting for the genuine joy of teaching and inquiry the weary drone of yellowed lecture notes and the rehashed conference paper written on the plane. An alternative stance is the cynical regard of one's position in the university as a sinecure from which lucrative forays may be made into the world of consulting. Both slave and cynic are deadly to the university.

Misrepresentation in inquiry

But in the great space of misrepresentation there are not just places in the daily life of academic governance, but in the intellectual life of teaching and learning. Some of these are vicious, that is they constitute deliberate attempts to lie and cheat. But most misrepresentations arise in a benign fashion, from a lack of awareness of what one is doing. Or, to put it in much broader and I think more reflective terms, an awareness of how concealing and unconcealing go on in any human inquiry as night follows day.

Vicious misrepresentation, such as deliberate lying and cheating, is quite rare in the academic world, where there is an enormous amount of trust, perhaps one of the glories of the university. Vicious misrepresentation, when brought from concealment to unconcealment, scandalizes as only a broken trust can. It starts with cancerous spots painted on mice, to miraculous finds of fossils in the Himalayas, and dribbles off to long and sleazy wrangles about whose samples were used to investigate the human immunodeficiency virus. In any field trust sometimes breaks down. You cannot be in a profession for 30 years without hearing about suspicions so strong that you "know" them to be true: data sets with outliers eliminated, for example, or even cobbled up wholesale to support a point. Unless an alert doctoral committee is tough enough to insist on evidence as to origin, it is virtually impossible to do anything about it later. The laws of libel are properly punitive, and you had better be sure rather than strongly suspicious. But tough insistence usually means that the taken-for-granted trust has already broken down, that the unthinkable has become thinkable. Yet even this may appear unreasonable, particularly when research has been conducted overseas. Perhaps the geologists have the right idea when they write into research proposals field checks – expensive, time-consuming, but trust worthy.

Sometimes misrepresentation occurs when one is enraptured by an ideological stance, makes obeisance to a claim to a fundamental truth, or clings to a method in which one has been intellectually potty-trained as a graduate student. All of these are instances of choosing a template, some "theoretical" framework, before one even approaches the particular topic of research.[22] Unless the template is totally absurd, perhaps of the type "There are no facts, the Holocaust did not really happen," it is usually quite possible to find something to fit it and make it reasonably plausible (Hard, 1987, p.21). After all, conceptual frameworks do, on occasion, allow us to bring

---

22 *The play on* template, *and the concealing shift brought about by* theoria's *change of place from the Greek to the Latin* contemplatio, *will not be pursued again. See Martin Heidegger's essay* Science and Reflection *(1977).*

something not seen, or seen only dimly, out of concealment. They also have a marked ability to conceal by lulling us into thinking that we are not only on the right track, but the only track for fully enlightened and perspicacious people like you and me to travel in our search for the deep structures of truth underlying the superficial appearances. So students – I use the term broadly – write on Third World countries knowing perfectly well that all the ills are due to the abhorrent colonial heritage, and an all-pervasive capitalist system. A system, by the way, that has become totally and thoughtlessly reified, and so becomes a splendid candidate for yet one more Devil theory of history. Sure enough, you look for what you want to find, the facts fit the case, the template works. One is tempted to tell stories about drunks looking for their wallets under the street lamp, because that is where the light is.

Differential potty training

Let me illustrate what I trust and hope is a non-vicious process of misrepresentation by two recent and quite concrete experiences; first, research on the diffusion of the AIDS epidemic, and, second, a two-week field trip to Jamaica, following a semester's seminar on the topic. The first I will not dwell on, since I have made the same comments elsewhere.[23] Sufficient to say that the mathematical modelling of the AIDS epidemic has been totally captured by what I can only call a differential Mafia. In 30 years of professional life, I do not think I have ever come across such closed, such thoroughly templated, potty-trained thinking. To model an epidemic you confine your thinking purely to the temporal domain – there is only a history, the spatial domain, the geography, literally never comes to thinking – and you reach up on the shelf for your favorite sets of differential equations. It helps if you started in the early Seventies doing what was purported to be "ecological systems modelling." This was all the rage then, funding was almost cornucopic, and everyone scratched everyone else's backs in the review process. Ten years

23 see Gould (1991)

later, some small boy at the National Science Foundation asked the naive question as to whether the modelling emperor was only muddling, and did he have any clothes on? Like a similarly embarrassing question for the opulently funded cloud seeding research two decades before, it was an unfortunate inquiry, pushed hard this time by real ecologists, who went out and looked at real ecological systems. As a result, funding for playing around in computerized sandboxes declined precipitously. No matter: it was ten years later, and the AIDS epidemic was beginning to pick up nicely. A sharp, sideways shift into the National Institutes of Health, and off we go again. One of the many high peaks of scientific insight now revealed is a purely temporal, 36-equation model of the diffusion of AIDS in New York (Blower et al., 1990). None of the equations can be properly parameterized, something which would require grubby empirical work best left to those behavioral scientists, not us theoreticians. After all, it is not our fault if empirical work cannot keep up with our theoretical advances. The sober fact that not one life has been saved, not one HIV transmission has been stopped, by the literally millions of dollars spent by NIH on this nonsense is apparently irrelevant, and certainly of no consequence. After all, what are National Institutes of Health for?[24]

Templating the third world

The second illustration identifies a larger, and much more pervasive theme as students – again I use the term broadly and as an honorific – who have not made the ontological distinction between shame and guilt, inquire about the conditions of the Third World. Here templating often plays a particularly excisionary role, slicing away all possibilities of seeing that do not fit the preconceptions. One is con-

---

24 *To those who would say that there is little point in criticizing unless you can put something better in its place (not a thesis I would hold to necessarily), I can only refer to the geographic conditions of spatio-temporal modelling, employing such approaches as Casetti's expansion method, Gorr's spatial adaptive filtering, and recent experiments with neural nets. For a more complete account see Chapter 12, "Time but no space: the failure of a paradigm", in my book* The Slow Plague: A Geography of the AIDS Pandemic *(1993).*

stantly reminded of Joseph de Maistre, of whom Isaiah Berlin (1991, p.162) wrote: "He is like a lawyer arguing to a brief: the conclusion is foregone ... for he is convinced of the truth, no matter what he may learn and encounter ... He ... is determined to carry his theories through, no matter what the evidence."

Acknowledging that a framework (template) may reveal as well as conceal, it is worth examining the marxist informed approach to illuminating conditions in the Third World. Recall that only a few decades ago such a perspective was hardly considered politically acceptable: today it has become almost the only politically correct, and that means *intellectually* acceptable, framework through which a student may approach Third World questions. Greatly simplifying the major arguments, though not I think to the point of parody, the ills of the Third World are fundamentally (Marxist are, after all, fundamentalists in the good old nineteenth century way),[25] the legacy of wicked colonial regimes and the continuing immoral and global capitalist system. In certain instances that should be carefully specified, colonial regimes did display wickedness. Unfortunately, wickedness is not the prerogative of colonial regimes: whatever instances may be listed, most of them pale in comparison with those available today in formerly colonial, but now independent countries, many of which have been independent for 30 years, surely enough time for the colonial legacy to fade? Many colonial regimes, in their administrative, judicial, and fiscal duties, displayed scrupulous honesty, and put into place highly bureaucratized systems of accounting

---

25 *It is this sort of fundamentalism, by definition a fundamentalism that remains obdurately uninformed for fear of contradicting itself, that lies at the heart of David Harvey's deep dislike of postmodern plurality. If you constantly and consistently make claims to the "only perspective," you must, simply to protect those claims, as well as your expressed belief that you have reached the ground of knowing, you must challenge, and do your best to dismiss, the tolerance and pluralism of postmodern perspectives. It seems to me that this was precisely the reason* The Condition of Postmodernity *was written, quickly, and with a strong reliance on secondary and tertiary texts, many of which were written and edited by those who were already in agreement with the template.*

that made it clear where personal responsibility lay.[26] Today we witness public corruption on scales never seen before in human history.[27] The colonial scapegoat is becoming less and less plausible as time goes by.

But then there is the immoral capitalist system, which is the other, and now primary cause of Third World misery. Surely no one can deny that it is wholly exploitative, that the profit motive drives all matters of humanity and decency from view. And the black heart of the system's immoral soul is the multinational company, playing off one weak Third World country against another in its search for tax relief, profit and power, greased by promises of employment, exports for hard currency, technical know how, and the "standard ten percent" to the national politicians. Zeus knows there are enough instances around, but few *with*in the *template* are willing to contemplate the idea that independent countries *do* have choices. Offers detrimental to a country's welfare can be refused, and initial terms can be negotiated and renegotiated.[28]

26 *I observed recently (1991) in Jamaica accounting procedures (chits, receipt books, signatures, multiple copies to check, etc.), identical to those I came across as a graduate student in Ghana more than 30 years ago (1959). In small matters, it remains very hard to cheat using public funds. In large matters, the sky seems to be the limit.*

27 *The Bokassas ($2 billion), the Mobutus ($5 billion), the Marcoses ($10 billion?), hardly seem worthwhile recalling anymore. But corruption is probably the best example of the "trickle down effect" we can find. Nigerian newspapers report $160 million stashed away by road contractors in two years; after most military coups those out of government, but in jail, are released as soon as some of the numbered accounts in Zürich are reassigned; while in the Caribbean, politicians with impeccable public credentials have increasingly large but private bank accounts in the Cayman Islands or "Zürich-by-the-Sea." These instances, and thousands of others, are extremely difficult to write about: first, because it is difficult to bring to light that which is deliberately concealed; second, because speaking or writing the truth means the journalist's visa is immediately revoked. As an example, see David Lamb's* The Africans *(1989), written in a few months upon his return from four years as a correspondent for the* Los Angeles Times. *It is truly an exposé, an overflowing after years of silence required in order to keep his reporter's credentials.*

28 *As Jamaica has done in a quite remarkable fashion with the aluminum companies. I shall comment further below, but there is a balance to be struck between no exploitation of large and rich reserves of natural resources, for which you have no foreseeable ability to exploit yourself (due to a lack of technique, a lack of energy to refine; and so on), and totally rapacious exploitation akin to national rape. You do not want to kill the goose that lays the aluminum egg, and if it accounts for a very high proportion of your international earnings skillful negotiation will have to cut the best deal you can get.*

A multinational in Jamaica

As a concrete instance, take the presence of ALCAN in Jamaica, mining bauxite and reducing it to alumina for refining in energy-rich places like Québec with large surpluses of cheap hydroelectric power. The 1947 laws, opening national (that is government owned) land to mining, specified that after the bauxite had been removed, the land should be restored to agricultural use.[29] In a now long and inevitably somewhat chequered history, some companies paid lip service only, some dragged their feet, and some, upon sitting down at an increasingly knowledgeable and tough negotiating table, decided to pull out. Some like Kaiser and ALCAN, and an international consortium in minority partnership with the Jamaican government (ALPART), decided to stay and work with and for Jamaica.

Perhaps writing "for Jamaica" brands one as a naive apologist, for within the template today it is inconceivable, a direct contradiction, that *any* multinational company might have a moral soft spot. Profit is the motive, and indeed ALCAN is a profitable company, including its Jamaican operations. If it were not, it could not exist, particularly in an industry in which the smallest technical edge may make the difference between making it or going under.[30] Yet I think this is a fair description. The land reclamation and agricultural program is, quite simply, enormously impressive. Top soil is scraped off an area to be mined (the bauxite lies often within a foot of the surface), and stored for future reclamation. The bauxite is extracted, and then the pits carefully graded back to slopes often less than the original contours. Over the now white limestone, a much richer base for agricul-

---

[29] *A long and complex story is being compressed here, but I think even in outline it remains a fair and truthful account.*

[30] *To go through the entire process from reserve estimation to final alumina reduction is to realize how extremely fine the cost margin is, and how risky the real, and not merely academic and theoretical, decision process is. Much bauxite lies in limestone "pockets," and must be carefully drilled to obtain a three-dimensional view of the various qualities of ore, which are then mixed to obtain exactly the standard for the particular alumina reduction process. This itself is so technically advanced that chemical engineers from rival companies are politely requested not to join educational and public relations tours of alumina plants for the well-founded fear that they will pick up, and exploit themselves "back home," the latest technical wrinkle that might be making a plant less than one percent more efficient.*

ture than the aluminum-rich bauxite,[31] the stockpiled topsoil is now spread and sowed in coarse grass to produce lush meadows.

On the basis of these pasture lands, ALCAN has developed what must surely be one of the most advanced and successful programs of agricultural research and production ever achieved in the tropics. It emphasizes dairy, as opposed to beef, production, on the grounds that milk is more nutritionally important for Jamaica's children than beef patties for the local Burger Kings. However, since cattle breeding is a gendered occupation, some beef is inevitably produced. Bull semen is still needed to impregnate cows, and calves are males roughly half the time. The result is that ALCAN now produces about a quarter of Jamaica's beef production, and a third of her milk production, backed by an intensive selective breeding program of the Jamaica Hope, a breed producing massive bulls displaying their Brahma heritage, and small, highly-heat resistant, and heavily milking cows. Semen is taken, prepared and stored with the latest preserving and cryogenic methods, and exported all over the tropical world for artificial insemination. Jamaica Hopes can produce a calf each year, while tropical heat reduces ovulation in temperate breeds and limits them to a calf once every 15-18 months. Since milk production is crucially dependent upon regular freshening, the Jamaica Hope outscores all other breeds under these conditions.

But, say the templaters, ALCAN obviously is not doing this for purely altruistic reasons. Already they are dominating and "taking over" Jamaica's milk and beef production, both high sources of protein. How does one answer this? If you do not want to see something, or if you want to see a hidden (deep structure?) motive, the real reason beyond the superficial appearance, there is little one can say. Except that this operation, like most others, is run entirely by Jamaicans; except to note that ALCAN is trying to "divest" itself,

---

[31] *The presence of bauxite close to the surface is often disclosed by a yellowing of the natural vegetation. Indeed such natural signs are often the tell-tale marks indicating where exploratory drilling for reserves might be undertaken. In contrast, a limestone "base" can often be made highly productive, as the Amish people in my own valleys of Pennsylvania know very well.*

not by pulling out, but by transferring more and more of the facilities and expertise to national hands. Generally, ALCAN has a high reputation and excellent relations in host countries. It undoubtedly pays them. But in what currency?

Seeing what you want to see

Sometimes the template is clear, even strident, in its presentation. Sometimes it discloses itself unwittingly within an institutionalized form and imprimatur. OXFAM, for example, with its impeccable moral and humanistic credentials, has published a report outlining for the general reader its efforts at supporting small scale development projects in the Caribbean (MacDonald, 1990). These include coffee and sewing cooperatives in Dominica, tool banks and literary centers in Haiti, and a farmer's association and a women's theater group in Jamaica. OXFAM is certainly doing good things. Yet one is left with an impression that virtually all of the misery of the Caribbean is externally imposed, that responsibility lies elsewhere; in the colonial legacy, and in the international economic system.

We start, for example, and one is tempted to say "as usual," with slavery, even though slavery was abolished over a century and a half ago in the Caribbean (with the exception of Puerto Rico, 1873, and Cuba, 1880). Nevertheless, there is a passage in the report about Haiti: "This is a tough, strong people ... that freed itself by force of arms from Napoleon's armies in 1804",[32] a romantic invocation that does nothing to enhance the image of the Caribbean's "poorest of the poor" after nearly 200 years of independence. "As usual" we have no hint that virtually every man, woman and child from Africa put into this appalling condition was hunted down, fettered and sold by fellow Africans, who, like the Greeks and their silver mines before them, regarded slavery as a normal human institution. Few wish to recall that no penetration of West Africa, from the minute trading enclaves along the coast, took place from 1482 until the 19th century, and that "the colonial era" lasted roughly 60-100 years,

---

32 MacDonald, 1990, p.19

years that came long after slavery had been abolished. This is neither an apologia for slavery or colonialism; it is a reminder that the attribution of all ills to these institutions should be carefully and openly thought about. For example, Caribbean fragmentation is due to the colonial whipping boy: "The divisions that exist within the Caribbean are the heritage of colonialism"[33] noting that there are no direct flights from English-speaking Jamaica to Spanish-speaking Dominica, only connections via Miami in the United States. No thought about potential traffic: one wonders who in Jamaica and Dominica would want such direct interaction, except executives of OXFAM with branches in both countries.

We continue with the second external cause: the exploitative capitalist system. Bauxite mining is presented in the report as mineral rape: "The industry is capital intensive and provides few jobs ... most of the smelting of the relatively cheap crude ore into high-value aluminum was done abroad",[34] and so on. But you cannot mine bauxite with picks, shovels and baskets-on-the-head, and smelting takes huge amounts of cheap energy, the very thing that bauxite producers do not have. Jamaica could "compete" with Norway in smelting only by importing yet more Venezuelan oil. Even the most obdurate templater who wants to see a different world would have to admit this would be sheer economic madness. In the last three years, we have seen, in eastern Europe and the former Soviet Union, exactly where romanticized price-setting leads.

Tourism is also excoriated: "Much tourist spending remains in the North ... (it) is notoriously volatile ... its social effect is to create a luxury enclave, predominately white in a background of poverty, predominately black" etc., but "The industry has become the main source of hard currency for Jamaica ... (although) Other territories with fewer natural resources ... have become even more dependent ... (some are) making an energetic bid for a greater share in the

---

33 MacDonald, 1990, p.49
34 MacDonald, 1990, pp.8-9

market".*35* So what do you do if you have little in the way of resources except sun and sand and blue water? Because what you do have is a tropical climate, tropical soils, and people. If you want to produce things and sell them to others, so you can buy things you want in return, you produce ... bananas, sugar, pimento, coffee, cocoa, ginger, citrus, tobacco ... what else? Rice was tried, and it did not work: it came out about twice as expensive as Guyanan. Well, what about industrialization? That might mean enclave production and free trade zones. But these cause other problems: "The model of development ... has had the reverse effect, by increasing balance of payment problems. Food imports have become a significant necessity ... There are other "knock on" effects. In Jamaica ... bauxite production aggravated an already serious land shortage ... agriculture languished and more and more people drifted to the cities in search of work".*36*

This is misrepresentation in its rawest form. Industrialization causes food imports; exploitative mining companies reduce the pittance of land available for farming, and drive people to the cities? No one says dietary habits for staple grains, wheat, maize and rice, mean almost 100 percent importation, the latter almost entirely from Guyana. No one says wheat is tough to grow in humid tropical conditions; no one says maize farming was tried, and produced maize at such an exorbitant cost that it was cheaper, much cheaper, to buy it from Iowa. As for rapacious mining companies driving poor farmers off the land and into the city, no one notes that *all* land in mining lease is government owned; that farming anywhere is increasingly regarded as hard, dirty, backbreaking work, not nearly as appealing as the beckoning bright lights of the city. As in most Third World countries, you cannot stop the flow to the cities, the moths to the candle flame. It does not take a wicked mining company to drive you to Kingston. On the contrary, any farmers displaced, a minute fraction of the national total, are carefully compensated today with new land, and funds and advice to set up again if they wish to. Many

35 MacDonald, 1990, p.9
36 MacDonald, 1990, p.10

do not.[37]

Again and again, the implication is always that the causes of the Caribbean's and Jamaica's misery and poverty are external. No one dares to mention as causal factors the internal "exploitation" of people by people; the lack of natural resources, particularly cheap forms of energy; and the now unthinkable problem, because it lies outside of the template, the neo-Malthusian "shibboleth" of too many people. People exploiting people is not an external problem, and is not going to be solved by any external pressures.[38] As for cheap energy, there is none.[39] Stand on Middle Peak (7,600 feet) at night and look down on Kingston and its more than one million people.[40] It is a blaze, a carpet of light. Over on your right hand are

[37] *Obviously, it would be silly to turn this into a paean of praise, for sometimes farmers leasing land are displaced as government-sanctioned and owned reserves are mined. But in renegotiations and reallocations of reserves carried out by the Jamaican government, carefully specified conditions were laid down to compensate farmers fully.*

[38] *Third World countries are going to have to solve the inequities of the distribution of national wealth themselves, and by whatever means they think best. No one seeing Kingston, Jamaica, can come away anything but appalled at the contrast between a relatively wealthy upper middle class driving new, highly-taxed, and very expensive cars, living in "Beverley Hills," right next to squatter settlements of the utmost physical squalor and human despair. These continue to grow no matter which political party is in power, political power expressed as graffitied boundaries dividing neighborhood from neighborhood without apparent rhyme or reason. Poor people from one politically defined neighborhood dare not enter the adjacent, and often just as poor, area of the rival party. Investigating this micro-geographic situation seems impossible because of the potential for violence. Even armed police are reluctant to enter certain areas of Kingston.*

[39] *Except a small amount of hydropower from small dams. It helps – anything helps – but essentially energy has to be imported. Nor do I see 100,000 biogas convertors as a practical solution. My guess is that eventually Jamaica will go atomic, once we move away technically from the dangerous light water reactor. Otherwise the lights will simply go out.*

[40] *Who knows how many? No one. The results of the 1980 census are still coming out, even as Jamaica prepares for another census in the early 90s. No census taker is going to enter certain areas of Kingston and get out alive. And if the results only appear by 2000, we shall have yet another exercise in historical demography, not a modern, future-oriented tool for social betterment. Because no one knows these basic population figures, no one has the faintest idea what birthrates, population increases, and the other usual statistics, are. As a result, the population of Kingston is "probably between 1 million and 2 million," and "probably between 50-60 percent of the total population." I often felt that a more reliable estimate of the birthrate could be achieved by simply walking through urban and rural areas, and counting the proportion of obviously pregnant young women compared to the total number of people passed, doing some elementary arithmetic, and making a good guess. Nothing in the official statistics could beat such an estimate.*

the smaller clusters of Ochos Rios, Montego Bay, Port Antonio, and so on. And then you think: every light bulb is shining with fossil energy captured millions of years ago in what is today Venezuela, Trinidad, even Nigeria. And every headlight too, and every truck, car, motorcycle moving. All imported energy. Bought with hard currency, i.e. currency that has some chance of keeping its value over the next few years, unlike your own whose value to others goes down and down because there is no confidence that anything substantial is backing it. This voracious appetite has nothing to do with the colonial heritage or capitalist exploitation. It is a choice made in a world already given.

Beyond the template: NeoMalthusianism

But the most unthinkable idea, and therefore least talked about, is the sheer, and I would say catastrophic, number of people, pressing in many islands of the Caribbean against an environment already in shock. Within the template this is not, and cannot be, a problem. It is only a figment of the capitalist imagination, and the problem requires only that the available resources are equitably distributed to be solved once and for all. In the OXFAM report it is not even mentioned as a cause of anything, yet it slips out again and again. Describing a farmer, we are told in passing "He is in his thirties, with nine children ... and five grandchildren",[41] while "Christina, mother of seven children, has been a weeder on (a Jamaican) sugar estate".[42] In Dominica, Altagracia tells us "I've got 11 children and 7 are married",[43] and in Haiti "Pressure on the soil increased after the French left in 1804 ... (land) was divided between the ex-slaves. Their descendants have become more and more crowded into smaller and smaller subdivided pieces",[44] while a photo in Haiti's mountains shows a once heavily forested slope as a devastated area,

---

41 MacDonald, 1990, p.7
42 MacDonald, 1990, p.23
43 MacDonald, 1990, pp.25-28
44 MacDonald, 1990, p.9

nothing but raw and deeply eroded gashes in the white limestone (MacDonald, 1990, p.12). Pressure on the soil ... from where? A Jamaican economist tells OXFAM "What we have in the Caribbean is lots of people. We don't have much else".[45] But from the context, the implication is that the International Monetary Fund is at fault. Even the huge tide of Jamaican immigration is seen as a result of Britain "urgently (needing) workers in the new national health service, in industry, and in the public system, and thousands of people ... answered the call".[46] No hint of too many people, just "lots of people ... answer(ing) the call," the "colonies" nobly answering the call of the Motherland.

What sort of a dream world is this? This is a country where the average age of a woman with her first child is probably around 15 (no one knows, or can know, for sure), mainly because bearing a baby is considered by young women to be a sign of status, a *rite de passage* into the adult world. It is a world where men sometimes boast they are "shooting for their half century" (their fiftieth child), so presumably they know how to keep track of both runs at a cricket match and the numbers of mothers and their children. It is a country where family planning is considered by many to be a joke, if they have heard of it at all. It is a society structured, that is literally connected, by a large number of sexual relations that make multiple partners commonplace. The local "Panther" condoms, even if they were free, are generally considered unreliable and irrelevant.[47] One woman, with a lifetime of social work and health care experience, was asked if she would take part in local family planning efforts, and categorically refused on the grounds that she saw no sense

---

45 MacDonald, 1990, p.15
46 MacDonald, 1990, p.14
47 In two weeks of careful observation, in both urban and rural areas, I saw only one, very small sign on the back of truck, "Two is better than too many," and two billboards with a chillingly fierce panther extolling protection, presumably from HIV, rather than pregnancy. With regard to HIV and AIDS, I see no hope, only ultimate human devastation. The unprotected sexual relations make a high-dimensional, tightly connected backcloth on which the HIV can exist and be transmitted as traffic. In many squatter areas there are no lights, unemployment is high (Hannah Town, Kingston, has 75 percent unemployment, MacDonald, 1990, p.13), and what is there to do but seek mutual pleasure in making love?

whatsoever to devoting her considerable energies to something upon which she could not make the slightest impact. There are a few family planning efforts: even in Catholic maternity hospitals workers in family planning come around asking if the women know about the various ways of avoiding pregnancy in the future. But they are, by and large, preaching to the converted. Who goes to a maternity hospital to have a child?

And so the people keep coming, and the pressures mount. On the environment, on immigration, on social and educational services, which increasingly no government can provide. But in phenomenological fashion, you have to try to enlarge the template to allow the condition of possibility of seeing, to be in that disclosive state so that things can come into language (Rorty, 1991b, p45). You have to let things be, you have to bring them into the open clearing where they are unconcealed. Where they can be re-presented in truth, and not concealed in mis-representation.

What I have re-presented in writing is true.

At least I think so.

For the moment.

References

Berlin I, 1991, "The Decline of Utopian Ideas in the West" in *The Crooked Timber of Humanity* (Alfred A. Knopf, New York)

Blower S, Hartel D, Dowlatabadi H, Anderson R and R May, 1990, "Drugs, Sex and HIV: A Mathematical Model for New York City", mss.

Gould P, 1991, "AIDS in Its Geographic Dimensions", in *Modelling the Geographic Diffusion of the AIDS Epidemic* American Association for the Advancement of Science, Washington, DC

Gould P, 1993 *The Slow Plague: A Geography of the AIDS Pandemic* (Blackwell, Cambridge, MA)

Hard G, 1987 *Storks and Children, Orchids and the Sun* (Walter de Gruyter, Berlin)

Harvey D, 1989 *The Condition of Postmodernity* (Basil Blackwell, Oxford)
Heidegger M, 1972 *On Time And Being* (Harper Torchbooks, New York)
Heidegger M, 1977, "Science and Reflection" in *The Question Concerning Technology and Other Essays* (Colophon Books, New YorkHarper) 155-182
Lamb D, 1989 *The Africans* (Mandarin, London)
MacDonald N, 1990 *The Caribbean: Making Our Own Choices* (OXFAM, Oxford)
Rorty R, 1991a *Objectivity, Relativism, and Truth: Philosophical Papers, Vol.I* (Cambridge University Press, Cambridge)
Rorty R, 1991b "Philosophy As Science, As Metaphor, and as Politics" in *Essays On Heidegger and Others: Philosophical Papers, Vol. 2* (Cambridge University Press, Cambridge)
Vattimo G and Rovatti P A (eds), 1983 *Il Pensiero Debole* (Feltrinelli, Milano)

Johann: Deux paysages alpins

THE MORAL POWER OF REPRESENTATION: RATIONALITIES, TRUST AND URBAN CONFLICT

by Ola Söderström

Introduction

In a chapter entitled *The Limits of Representation*, Michel Foucault (1973, pp.217-249) situates the beginning of the movement which was to free the order of our knowledge from the domination of representative discourse at the end of the eighteenth century, i.e. at the end of what he calls the Classical Age. It is from this moment on that, progressively, the order of things will no longer be confined to the space of its representation, but will have to be sought in the realm of the invisible:
"In order to find a way back to the point where the visible forms of beings are joined – the structure of living beings, the value of wealth, the syntax of words – we must direct our search towards that peak, that necessary but always inaccessible point, which drives down, beyond our gaze, towards the very heart of things" (Foucault, 1973, p.239).
Hence, the limits of representation, as an epistemological question, correspond, or so it would appear, to a stage in the development of our knowledge. It seems to have a historical grounding because, from the end of the eighteenth century onward, the space of representation finds itself unable to contain the essence of that which is represented: "the very being of that which is being represented is now going to fall outside representation itself".[1] Nevertheless, in Foucault's view, it is only the "empirical sciences" that will free themselves from representation during a period which will witness the emergence of the human sciences. Indeed, the human sciences are fully situated in the space of representation as representation

---

[1] Foucault, 1973, p.240. This does not of course mean that representation – as well as the materiality of representation – no longer plays a role in the production of scientific facts...

itself constitutes "the general pedestal of that form of knowledge, the basis that makes it possible".[2]

Heidegger (1962, p.89), as we know, saw this advent of the human sciences ("anthropologies") as Descartes's supreme triumph. That is to say, the primacy of representation in the human sciences which is evoked by Foucault, finds, according to him, its condition of possibility in the Cartesian equation between truth and "the certainty of representation"(Heidegger, 1962, p.79). Thus, with Descartes, we enter the "age of the world as picture" – whereas neither the medieval world nor the ancient world had existed as "picture" – and this is achieved according to a double process which makes the world a conceived picture and man, a *subjectum*. Descartes's position itself has however "as a presupposition the metaphysics of Plato and Aristotle" (Heidegger, 1962, p.89). For the world to become picture it was necessary, in accordance with the Heideggerian reading of ancient Greece, that man should change, and that rather than being a "hearer of being" (Parmenides), he should have a mode of access to the world which is primarily visual (Plato) (Heidegger, 1962, p.82).[3] This shift thus constitutes the distant condition of the Modern Times as the time of representation.[4]

The limits of representation are thus not a chapter in the history of ideas, but indicate – and this is now a truism – the limits of our knowledge. Consequently, there is probably no better place to throw into question the limits of representation than that place where knowledge as representation is faced with the resistance of that which is represented; in other words, a place where the performative ability of knowledge, i.e. the power exerted on the body and its practices, is sufficiently manifest and intrusive to be challenged. In this respect, as Sylvia Ostrowetsky points out (1982, p.5), urbanism constitues a privileged field of investigation as it is both "anthro-

---

[2] Foucault, 1973, p.363. In effect, for Foucault, the concepts which are mobilized by this knowledge – meaning, norm, rule, conflict, etc. – all originate in representation. See pp.361-364.

[3] Ibid., p.82.

[4] Representation is defined here as "bringing before oneself by drawing to oneself" (Heidegger, 1962, p.83).

pology" – insofar as it is replenished by the human sciences – *and* "management of the social body."

All institutionalized knowledge – for example, statistics – is of course a mode of management of the social body; what is nevertheless specific to urbanism is the visible and physical character of this management, a fact which explains why it constitutes an object of conflict to a degree considerably more important than statistics.[5] The extraordinary violence that the practice of urbanism potentially entails thus finds its counterforce in the potential resistance of the bodies and minds that this discipline means to manage. It is into this conflictual relation between one form of knowledge – and thus representations – and its object that I intend to situate my exploration of the limits of representation in this paper. This investigation is to be more pragmatic than speculative in the sense that the reflections that I here propose on our common theme of discussion find their origins in an analysis of urban conflicts, which has been carried out in the context of a research project and not in an examination posed at the outset as purely theoretical.[6]

The interpretation that I am trying to give to these urban conflicts is oriented towards understanding them in terms of conflicting rationalities. This standpoint involves the study of the way the different urban actors approach a specific planning issue by using different techniques of representation, different methods of evaluation and different strategies of legitimation to justify their approach. Urban conflicts are, of course, determined to a large extent by economic and political processes and interests that are now well documented in urban research, but their more cognitive dimension has seldom been explored. If I claim that the "constructivist" analysis of this cognitive dimension is important, it is not only because of its relative autonomy in the planning process but also because these economic and political interests tend to be dissolved in the apparent

---

[5] *This does not of course imply that statistics is an inferior tool as far as this task is concerned.*

[6] *This research is being funded by the Fonds National Suisse de la Recherche Scientific in the context of The National Programme of Research 25: "City and Transport."*

neutrality of the techniques of representation traditionally used.[7] A number of planning tools (technical expertise among others) function indeed like "black boxes" that neutralize these interests not only in the eyes of the ordinary citizen but often also in the eyes of their users (planners, architects or politicians). The efficiency of this process of neutralization is due to the fact that these techniques are very often taken for granted by their users; they are in a sense what "everybody knows". They are what their users, as specialists of urban matters, have learnt at university and this training is itself situated in the continuum of a more general context of socialization dominated by a specific conception of rationality. In other words the power of these techniques lies in their consistency with Rationality with a capital R, that is, rationality defined as a systematic, explicit and consistent reasoning building on a disengaged perspective and claiming universal relevance. This consistency of routinely-used techniques of representation in planning with this definition of rationality renders them to a large extent auto-legitimizing. Rationality is thus at the origin of a legitimate representation of a planning issue, a Representation with a capital R, and this Representation functions in urban matters as one of the bases of the authority of authorities.[8] Thus the legitimacy of urbanism as a means of managing the social body is based on the evidence of this Representation.[9]

In other words, it is not simply a matter of asserting, as we have said, that our rationality is representation – and representation that is a calculus, to be certain (Heidegger, 1962, p.96) – and thus that representation in itself is already content; rather, once this is admitted, it is a matter of examining how that which we have designated as Representation today in-forms town planning practices. Now,

---

7 For an analysis of the social power of representations, see the essays collected in G. Fyfe and J. Law (1989) and in M. Lynch and S. Woolgar (1988).

8 Needless to say, there are of course other sources for this authority, be it only the legitimacy acquired in a democracy through voting procedures. But it is the autonomous power of routinely-used techniques of representation which I am trying to isolate here.

9 For an analysis of the "fixation of visual evidence" in the context of experimental science, see K. Amann and K. Knorr-Cetina (1988).

Representation and Rationality are in a state of crisis in the field of urbanism as elsewhere and a tradition of urbanistic criticism already exists.[10] To begin with, it will thus be necessary to briefly discuss certain elements of the debate on rationality in order to understand the persistence of a dominant rationality.

In the case study on which we base most of this paper, however, the validity of the Representation is contested by a group of inhabitants of a central urban area where an administrative centre should replace a 19th century residential neighbourhood. Consequently I shall be interested, in the latter part of this paper, in *how* and *why* this Representation is challenged and then in the consequences of this criticism for the evolution of this urban conflict. By consequences, I mean in particular the reaction of the planners to this criticism which is, as we will see, formulated in moral terms. This observation will lead me, in concluding, to develop an analogy between this planning problem and the experiments imagined by Harold Garfinkel precisely to explore the link between morality and cognition.

In other words, two excursuses will be of use in this paper: before coming to the problem of *how* and *why* a Representation reaches a kind of limit in the specific case of an urban conflict, I shall introduce an excursus which deals with the notion of rationality, and then, before proposing an interpretation of some of the consequences of this conflict, another digression will be necessary on the notion of trust.

The tenaciousness of Rationality

In Western thought two dominant versions of the discourse on modernity exist side by side: a heroic one celebrating the successes of a rationalization of society and a critical one condemning the same process in the name of its societal, human or spiritual costs. Both versions share however the same diagnosis of modernity: modernity is the history of the triumph of Rationality. So even if the

---

[10] Among other works, cf. Breheny and Hooper (1985) and of course Olsson (1980).

first version is a positive and the second one a critical account of the evolution of our modes of thought and social organization, both stories tend to bear a good deal of resemblance to each other.

In other words, modernity as the triumph of Rationality – be it qualified as instrumental, strategic or in any other terms – is described in both versions of the discourse on modernity as an evolutionary and all-pervading process. This is no doubt a convincing story.[11] The existence of a dominant rationality is indeed difficult to contest, and the best proof of the triumph of a universalistic conception of rationality lies perhaps in the fact that many of its most radical critics cannot escape thinking in its terms, dividing means of reasoning between Rational and irrational ones. For Lyotard, for instance, but also for other French critics of modernity, the only alternative to Rationality seems to be absurdity (Toulmin, 1991, p.241). Practical reason or, to use another term, the reasonableness of everyday action is apparently most often unworthy of being labeled rational. Rationality has thus imposed its own language on the reflection on rationality.

So if the account of modernity as the triumph of Rationality is convincing, it also tends to obscure the fact that rationality is plural and not only in the nostalgic erudition of the anthropologist or the historian of science but also today in the heart of the modern Western world.

No doubt this plurality has been recognized thanks to studies that developed in at least three fields of research: cultural anthropology, the history and sociology of science and comprehensive sociology. In effect, and though it is not yet closed – and will probably never be – the discussion in cultural anthropology concerning the rationality or irrationality of beliefs and actions in primitive societies has very seriously shaken the conception of a unified and universal rationality (Wilson, 1970; Hollis and Lukes, 1982). In the history and sociology of science, the studies of Alasdair MacIntyre (MacIntyre, 1988) on the rationality of pre-modern traditions, the description of

---

11 *Especially when the evolution of knowledge is embedded in its social and political context as in Stephen Toulmin's recent account of the emergence and progressive deconstruction of what he calls the "scaffolding of modernity" (Toulmin, 1991).*

the reduction of rationality in the 17th century by Stephen Toulmin (Toulmin, 1991) and the analyses of Bruno Latour on science in action (Latour, 1984, 1987) constitute among others – and from different angles – very efficient attacks on the same target. Schematically speaking, these different studies have shown that science in the making is much more irrational than what it claims to be (Latour, 1987), that there is no Great Divide between modern Western culture and irrational/magical thought (MacIntyre, 1988), that other cultures function according to context-dependent conceptions of rationality (Winch 1970; Lukes, 1970), and that alternative types of rationality also govern human conduct and thinking in the contemporary Western world (Goffman, 1974; Garfinkel, 1967).

But the problem is that this critical debate on the forms of rationality is to a large extent confined to academia and has thus very little impact on practical social life. The idea of a plurality of rationalities has seldom penetrated the procedures of social regulation, and it thus has a very limited influence in matters of urban planning: rationality in its universalistic and abstract form, despite the fact that we now know its relative irrelevance for the understanding of human behaviour, still governs the functioning of social institutions. So, even if this domination, with its correlative distinction between respectable and non-respectable modes of thought, may loosen its grip within academic circles, it is far from being the case outside of them.

More than just an observation of how Rational planning has endured despite various criticisms that have been levelled at it, the upcoming analysis will attempt to provide an explanation which may prove to be somewhat unconventional.

Norms, Rationality and insiders

The domination of Rational procedures in urbanism has meant that, in most cases, universal and abstract norms and techniques of representation are routinely applied to planning issues. The analysis of an operation which is currently under way in the town of Lausanne, Switzerland allows us to observe how these procedures of construction and representation of the object are utilized. It also allows us to take note of the discrepancies between this representation and the construction and representation of inhabitants of the area as collected by semi-directed interviews.

The planning area is constituted by a small set of buildings, mostly housing, situated in the central part of Lausanne. It is characterized by the presence of a high amount of foreigners, by a predominance of unskilled workers plus a few students and social workers, and by – according to Swiss standards – a fairly high degree of social interaction, owing to the presence of several cafes, shops and cultural activities.

The planners' approach to the area in question in Lausanne is characterized by a number of features:

• the area is bounded by clear spatial limits determined by the extension of the operation planned. In terms of my former discussion of Rationality, a zenithal – and thus disengaged – point of view is privileged;

• the urbanistic project planned in this area is defined in terms of desirable forms and functions of the future construction on the *tabula rasa* of the architect's blank sheet. Cleared of the sediments of meaning and practice, the area can be the object of a de-contextualized project;

• and finally, the choice between keeping the present residential buildings or constructing an administrative centre is justified by a general discourse on the proper situation for housing (the area is considered as inappropriate for housing) and by an evaluation of the quality of infrastructures. In order to objectify the rejection of a solution in terms of rehabilitation, an expertise was used for the evaluation of the state of buildings and of the costs of rehabilitation. This expertise consists primarily of a codification of an existing building relative to what is held as a standard state of the infrastructures and standard norms of comfort and then of an evaluation of the costs of rehabilitation on the basis of the difference between the analyzed building and a standard building.[12]

---

12 The standards used in this expertise, called MER, which can be applied to all pre-war

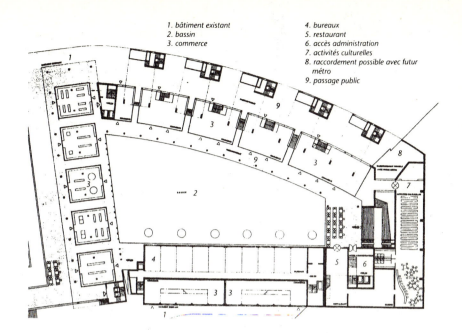

Figure 1: The project

These are in other words the main attributes – or "black boxes" – of the normal representation of the object. This representation gets its legitimacy and its capital R not only from the figure of the expert who constructs it but because the rationality of the project is conceived in universal and abstract terms and thus the practical reason of the planners moulds itself in the procedures of Rationality. But it could have been otherwise, the project could also have been conceived from the start according to another criterion of rationality, for instance as "relative to its reception by the persons concerned by the project",[13] and this would have led to a context-dependent, non-reproducible representation. This does not mean of course that there are no other reasons behind the choice of this approach; there is for

---

buildings in Switzerland, derive from an analysis of 6,000 buildings. See Vicari and Mermillod (1989).

13 A conception of rationality which was, as Toulmin (1991) reminds us, in current use before the scientific revolution of the 17th century.

example the problem of scale: de-contextualisation is indeed not only due to an autonomy of Representation but must also be accounted for in terms of the specific task of planners which is to look beyond the local scale and to consider more global interests. But if there are other driving forces behind the use of these techniques that may reinforce them, what is important to notice is the overall consistency of this procedure with Rationality. These techniques of representation can thus be trusted because they correspond to the rationally-sanctioned understanding of urban matters and because they consist of routinely-used structures of interpretation of the urban reality.

In spite of this, and for the reasons mentioned in the introduction, this type of project sometimes meets with opposition. In this case the inhabitants of the area were aware of the consequences of the realization of this project: they knew that they would have to leave a cheap, centrally located area as the residential buildings would be replaced by administrative ones. Opponents of the project attacked the planners' project construction methods, contesting the planners' representational authority on the grounds that they were outsiders; opponents also argued that the particular value of the neighbourhood was to be found in its being a site of social interaction and held that comfort norms did not take into account differences in needs. Different publications were thus diffused in which they assert the specificity of their neighbourhood versus the decontextualised definition of the planners (in terms of abstract forms and functions) and the specificity of their needs versus the standard and universal norms used by the planners.

However, between 1988 and 1991 this opposition remained the doing of a small group of people: this was then an instance, as is often the case in similar situations, of appropriation of "the residents' collective voice" by a small group claiming to speak on its behalf. In order to verify if in fact it was legitimate to speak of a conflict of rationalities, it was thus necessary to carry out in-depth interviews with both those inhabitants involved in the project and those who were opposed to it. What the analysis of these interviews demonstrates is how difficult it was for the inhabitants to conceive of their environment in a disengaged, decontextualised and universal manner: they are insiders and as such they are reluctant to effectuate one of the basic tasks of a Rational attitude, i.e. the suspension of subjectivity.

The difficulty that insiders had representing their neighbourhood in a disengaged manner was perhaps best demonstrated during the interviews when the inhabitants were asked to define their neighbourhood in spatial terms: when asked to describe discursively the boundaries of their neighbourhood, the task was first perceived as abstract and difficult. Most of them told the interviewer to reformulate the question and, of course, no one was able to provide an immediate answer in terms of the clear-cut limits of the planning maps. But later in the interview when aspects of their daily life were discussed, different boundaries were formulated which corresponded to different aspects of social and spatial practices.

The diversified limits are determined by day-to-day activities (the frequenting of public places, shopping as well as the network of children's friends ...), thereby making of this neighbourhood a socio-spatial construct, i.e. a qualified space. What we have here is thus another type of practical reason at work but one which is far from corresponding to the code of Rationality. In this sense this urban conflict is not only a conflict between economic interests or different conceptions of the future of a central urban area but also a conflict of rationalities. Different rationalities and different cognitive positions are in competion in this urban operation. A normal Representation founded on the procedures of Rationality is challenged by the engaged practical reason of the inhabitants opposed to the project.

Having briefly looked at how the limits of a Representation can be established when its object resists, I will now turn to an analysis of what happens when the legitimacy of the Representation is thus called into question.

What happened, in fact, in the specific case under study is a breakdown of communication. As might be expected, when opponents and planners met they did not speak the same language and could not find a common ground for discussion. Even more interest-

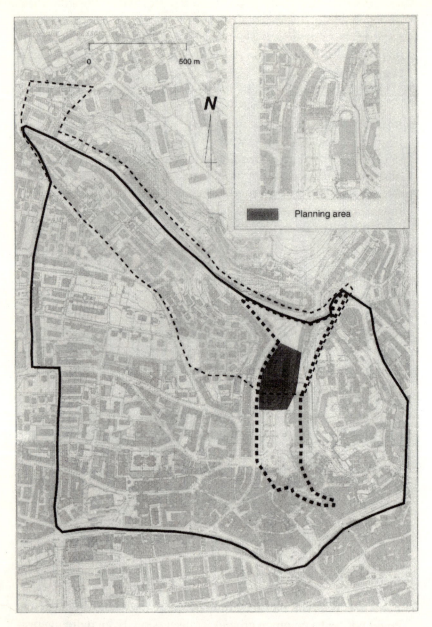

Figure 2: Different identities of the neighbourhood[14]

ing, though, was the hostile attitude of the planners: it was not only that they could not really *under*stand the challenge made to their procedures but they also simply couldn't stand it. This was obvious in the accounts given by the different participants in those meetings where the dialogue came to a quick halt. It also appeared very clearly in the interviews in which the planners took part: each time the interviewer reported as neutrally as possible the oppositions of the inhabitants, the planners, architects and politicians involved in the project changed the register of their speech and forgot their formal and polite (Swiss) manners. Their reaction was both aggressive and moralizing in the sense that the opponents were condemned for not understanding what was good for them: a clear sentiment of frustration in front of what was considered as ingratitude was thus expressed by the different persons responsible for the project.

The problem here is of course not one of "good" inhabitants being confronted with "bad" and aggressive bureaucrats, so what is it? What can the link between Representation and moral judgement be? An author, Harold Garfinkel, has tried to elaborate on this link in a way that seems relevant for the interpretation of these types of conflicts.

But here again, before developing this, I must clarify my standpoint. I do not claim that this attitude is systematic in all urban conflicts – different types of community planning have been experimented with all over the world and have pacified urban issues to a greater or lesser extent. Neither do I claim that procedures of planning in Switzerland are particularly brutal and bureaucratic. They are instead very prudent, constantly making an effort to anticipate any kind of opposition in order to prevent conflict. But what is interesting is that they still very often fail to do so, and my suggestion is that this failure is linked to the power of taken-for-granted repre-

---

14 These different modes of identification of the neighbourhood have been reconstructed from elements of discursive information taken from a part of the interviews involving the inhabitants of the neighbourhood. Paradoxically, I am here using a cartographic representation to depict non-cartographic rationalities... This stands of course as the best demonstration not only of the power of maps, but more generally of that of visual communication, which Ivins (1969) discusses.

sentations. So if I think that this particular problem encountered in my case-study is worth some effort of interpretation, it is because it provides evidence that "new" and sophisticated paradigms in planning theory – as for instance John Friedmann's Transactive Planning which aims at a dialogue between different dimensions of knowledge and different cognitive positions – underestimate the moral power of representation.

Trust and the consequences of distrust in urban conflicts

In the case of this planning conflict in Switzerland, I would suggest that the reaction of the planners to the opposition formulated by the inhabitants is analogous to the reactions to an attitude of distrust in ordinary interaction as described in Harold Garfinkel's "breaching experiments". A digression on the ethnomethodological project as formulated by Garfinkel is here necessary to legitimate this analogy.

The theoretical sources of Garfinkel's ethnomethodology are twofold: on one hand there is Talcott Parsons's theory of action, on the other, Alfred Schütz's comprehensive sociology. Being confronted with the imponent architecture of Parsons's theory of action was partly due to biographical reasons insofar as Garfinkel began his academic career in the 1940's at Harvard's Department of Social Relations, and Parsons was at that time the head of the Department. Garfinkel quickly expressed dissatisfaction with several of Parsons's assumptions and concepts. In particular, he was dissatisfied with Parsons's conception of the rationality of action which "involves a comparison between the actor's knowledge and the putatively complete and accurate knowledge possessed by the scientific observer" (Heritage, 1984, p.24). If, according to Parsons, the reasons for an action are not "understandable and verifiable by positive empirical science",[15] then the action is to be considered non-rational and should be interpreted as the result of the internalization of social norms. Garfinkel's main criticism of this conception of rational action is that it discards the actor's own knowledge and interpretation

---

15 *Parsons quoted by Heritage (1984, p.24).*

of the situation, reducing him/her to what he calls a "judgemental dope". Parsons's conception is problematic, according to Garfinkel, because it draws attention from what the latter calls the "reasonableness of actions" in the common-sense world and that I may call, with reference to my former discussion of rationality, practical, local or context-dependent rationalities. Instead of being marginal to an understanding of Hobbes's problem of social order as it is in Parsons's position, the reasonableness of action is thus central for Garfinkel.

Clearly Garfinkel did not deny the moral power of norms but thought that it was to be explored and understood within the common-sense world of everyday life. Schütz's conception of the lifeworld and of what he called the "attitude of daily life" – being one of the only theoretical sources available at the time – became for Garfinkel the second theoretical background for his researches as he tried to grasp the link between morality and common-sense interpretations of the world or, in other words, between morality and cognition.

It was in this theoretical context that Garfinkel developed his breaching experiments or his experiments with trust in the 1950's and 1960's. The idea of these experiments is stated very simply by Garfinkel in the introduction to his famous paper on his experiments with trust:

"In accounting for the persistence and continuity of the features of concerted actions, sociologists commonly select some set of stable features of an organization of activities and ask for the variables that contribute to their stability. An alternative procedure would appear to be more economical: to start with a system of stable features and ask what can be done to make for trouble. The operations that one would have to perform in order to produce and sustain anomic features of perceived environments and disorganized interaction should tell us something about how social structures are ordinarily and routinely being maintained" (Garfinkel, 1963, p.187).

One of Garfinkel's hypotheses for these experiments was that a person does not only respond to the perceived social environment around him (that is the feelings, behaviour, relationships that he is confronted with) but also to the perceived *normality* of these events (Garfinkel, 1963, p.188). Before experimenting with this normality and trying to create trouble and confusion in an ordinary interaction, Garfinkel had then to define the conditions of normality, i.e. the attributes of a "common-sense environment". Following but also completing Schütz's definition of the attitude of daily life, he identified a series of features describing this common-sense environment. Each of these features is expected to be known and respected by the different participants in an interaction. As a consequence trust is used by Garfinkel in his rather peculiar language "to refer to a person's compliance with the expectancies of the attitude of daily life as a morality" (Garfinkel, 1967, p.50). The idea of his breaching experiments was then of course to break this trust by violating one or several of these expected features of a normal interaction in a situation that a subject was supposed to perceive as an ordinary daily life situation and not as an experiment or a game.

In his paper, Garfinkel refers to different and more or less sophisticated experiments. I shall report only one of them because of its relevance to the analysis of the moral attitude of the planners in confrontation with the opposing inhabitants in the urban conflict analyzed here.

In one experiment, the indication given to the experimenters was "to engage an acquaintance or friend in an ordinary conversation and, without indicating that what the experimenter was saying was in any way out of the ordinary, to insist that the person clarify the sense of his commonplace remarks" (Garfinkel, 1963, p.221).

One of the experimenters (in fact essentially Garfinkel's students), a woman, reported the following interaction:

"On Friday night my husband and I were watching television. My husband remarked that he was tired. I asked, "How are you tired? Physically, mentally or just bored?"
S: "I don't know, I guess physically, mainly."
E: "You mean that your muscles ache, or your bones?"
S: "I guess so. Don't be so technical."
S: (After more watching) "All these old movies have the same kind

of old iron bedstead in them."
E: "What do you mean? Do you mean all old movies, or some of them, or just the ones you have seen?"
S: "What's the matter with you? You know what I mean."
E: "I wish you'd be more specific."
S: "You know what I mean! Drop dead!"(Garfinkel, 1963, p.221)

For Garfinkel this experiment was aimed at violating one of the assumptions of a normal interaction which is the "congruency of relevances". This assumption is for Schütz, in his general thesis of "reciprocal perspectives", one of the idealizations necessary for a possible intersubjectivity. If the congruency of relevances is breached here it is because the experimenter does follow the normal rules of the game: he does not suspend his subjectivity, or differently put by Garfinkel he does not "interpret the actually and potentially common objects in an 'empirically identical' manner that is sufficient for the purposes at hand" (Garfinkel, 1963, p.220). What happens is that the experimenter does not respect one of the taken-for-granted assumptions of everyday interaction by not drawing upon background knowledge of "what everybody knows" (Heritage, 1984, p.81).

One important aspect of these experiments is their consequence for the interaction. On one hand they resulted in most cases in a rapid and complete breakdown of the communication – as in the "drop dead!" of the above example – and, on the other hand, the experimenters were morally sanctioned by the subjects for not respecting the rules (Heritage, 1984, p.81). Hostility was rapidly shown by the subjects and the experimenters were summoned to explain their behaviour which was considered as nasty and illegitimate. The moral response to this non-compliance with rules is in Garfinkel's opinion to be explained by the importance of trust: if there is no trust in social interaction there is no possibility of social order.

The point I want to make is now fairly obvious: it is that the hostility of planners and their moral condemnation of the opponents is to be understood as a reaction to an attitude of distrust. The rejection of the normal representation of a planning operation as formulated by the authorities breaches the assumption of a congruency of relevances: the inhabitants implicitly argue, as my analysis of conflicting rationalities tried to show, that the object they are talking about is different. It does not have the spatial boundaries of the official planning documents and is not constituted by a set of functional and morphological attributes. It is instead an object constructed by their spatial and social practices, by their memory of past events in the neighbourhood, by the presence of friends or enemies in the area, by their routinely accomplished activities in and around the area, etc. If they are morally condemned it is thus for refusing to adopt a Rational, disengaged perspective and for not adhering to the techniques of representation routinely used to promote and translate the common good.

But this is not the only expectancy breached by the inhabitants. It could also be argued that they violate the assumption of the "interchangeability of standpoints" which constitutes the other idealization in Schütz's general thesis of "reciprocal perspectives" documented by Garfinkel in his experiments. As formulated by Schütz it is the assumption that "I take it for granted – and assume that my fellow man does the same – that if I change places with him so that his 'here' becomes mine, I shall be at the same distance from things and see them with the same typicality as he actually does".[16] To breach this assumption students were asked by Garfinkel to enter a store, to select a customer, and to treat the customer as a clerk without giving any hint that it could be otherwise or that the situation was abnormal in any way. An analogous violation is at work in my case-study insofar as the inhabitants did not recognize the special status of the planners as experts of the urban environment disputing among other things the validity of their technical expertise and rejecting implicitly their claim to a "special" and hierarchically superior approach to urban matters.

In other words, what is disputed by the opponents to the project is the taken-for-grantedness of the normal procedures of Rational planning: they reject the assumption that the traditional schemes of

16 Schütz quoted by Heritage (1984, p.55).

representation and interpretation of the urban reality should be applied to their situation and thus to all situations.

The analogy between everyday interaction and urban planning is I think legitimate insofar as normal procedures of urban planning have become naturalized to the point where they function as a fundamental assumption of the interaction between different urban actors in a planning process. As a consequence, the violation of this assumption, i.e. an attitude of distrust, is likely to produce a breakdown in the dialogue between urban actors because of the moral issues associated with the compliance with interaction rules. To show the limits of Representation here is thus to show distrust and to be exposed to moral condemnation.

It appears then that the criticism of Rationality which has given rise to an increased consciousness of the limits of Representation do not hinder the exercise of its moral power in the crucial area that the processes of social regulation constitute.

In developing this speculative interpretation of a planning process my aim has not been of course to propose any kind of general theory of urban conflicts. I have instead tried to understand the inertia and power of Rational Representations of the urban environment by looking at a point of friction, a point where they are not taken for granted, where their limits are signified. If the emphasis has been put on a case-study it is because I think that the power of Representation is best unveiled when it becomes performative, when it is considered with regard to its practical consequences. It is there that Representation can be stripped of its guise of neutrality and appear as a highly moral accomplishment.

References

Amman K and Knorr-Cetina K, 1988, "The fixation of (visual) evidence" in *Representation in Scientific Practice* Eds M Lynch and S Woolgar (Routledge, London) pp 85-121.

Breheny M, Hooper A (Eds), 1985 *Rationality in Planning, Critical Essays on the Role of Rationality in Urban and Regional Planning* (Pion, London)

Foucault M, 1973 *The Order of Things* (Random House, New York)

Fyfe G, Law J (Eds), 1989, "Picturing Power, Visual Depictions and Social Relations" *Sociological Review Monograph*, no 35, University of Keele

Garfinkel H, 1963, "A conception of, and experiments with, 'trust' as a condition of stable concerted actions" in *Motivation and Social Interaction* Ed. O J Harvey (Ronald Press, New York) pp 187-238

Garfinkel H, 1967 *Studies in Ethnomethodology* (Prentice-Hall, Englewood Cliffs)

Goffman E, 1974 *Frame Analysis* (Harper, New York)

Heidegger M, 1962, "L'époque des 'conceptions du monde'" in *Chemins qui ne mènent nulle part* (Gallimard, Paris)

Heritage J, 1984 *Garfinkel and Ethnomethodology* (Polity Press, Cambridge)

Hollis M, Lukes S, 1982 *Rationality and Relativism* (Basil Blackwell, Oxford)

Ivins W, 1969 *Prints and Visual Communication* (The MIT Press, Cambridge)

Latour B, 1984 *Les microbes, guerre et paix* (Métailié, Paris)

Latour B, 1987 *Science in Action. How to Follow Scientists and Engineers through Society* (Harvard University Press, Cambridge)

Lukes S, 1970, "Some Problems about Rationality", in *Rationality* Ed. B Wilson (Basil Blackwell, Oxford)

Lynch M, Woolgar S (Eds), 1988 *Representation in Scientific Practice* (Routledge, London)

MacIntyre A, 1988 *Whose Justice? Which Rationality?* (Duckworth, London)

Olsson G, 1980 *Birds in Egg/Eggs in Bird* (Pion, London)

Ostrowetsky S, 1982, "La représentation et ses doubles", texte présenté à l'occasion de la Table ronde internationale sur les représentations, Lyon, 17-20 décembre 1982 (mimeo)

Toulmin S, 1991 *Cosmopolis – La nascita, la crisi e il futuro della modernità* (Rizzoli, Milano)

Vicari J, Mermillod P, 1989 *Manuel MER, Méthode d'Evaluation Rapide des coûts de remise en état de l'habitat* (Chancellerie de la Confédération Suisse, Berne)

Wilson B (Ed), 1970 *Rationality* (Basil Blackwell, Oxford)

Winch P 1970, "Understanding a primitive society", in *Rationality* Ed B Wilson (Basil Blackwell, Oxford)

DO YOU THINK COLUMBUS COULD HAVE BEEN A WOMAN?

by Verena Meier

Children in Bocas de Satinga, Colombia

Part I: Histories starting in ancient Greece

After all I have heard and thought so far, what I want to do here is to ask about voice. About her voice, and, more specifically, about feminist geography and some of the questions arising from it.

The choice of this topic has not been very difficult for me, because it is urgent. Which does not mean that actually talking about it is not difficult, as things can also be too important, too close. Understanding comes out of that tension given through distance. Also, I sense that communicating now might be to solidify further, and to hold captured, what is desperately trying to become fluid and free. Nevertheless, I will talk about women and feminist aims in geography.

Nevertheless, I will talk about women and feminist aims in geography.

I want to talk about public space filled with dissonant noises and action. Let me first remind you that my country (Switzerland) is an old democracy with a high degree of federalism and direct participation of its citizens, and a country also very fond of its great variety of local folklore. It is part of this folklore, and also local civil rights that in the Canton of Appenzell Innerrhoden women were not allowed to vote on their local state issues up to the year of 1990. What does this have to do with human geography?

I hope it explains, why I stress action rather than calm. I guess it does hint about some of the contradictions enlightened science and its applications have produced; and, more central to my argument, it proves the importance of folklore and of publicity. Japanese and U.S. TV people came to Appenzell – what more does business want there?

Try for a smile. No, I will not bother you with exercises in discriminational analysis. We cannot afford to be that naive about tools that have been used and ab-used by others. We cannot afford to be naive about language in general.

What I really want to tell you about is a warm air that I feel blowing through the windows and fissures of that old building called Science, with all its institutional frameworks and theoretical monuments. Some of the windows had to be opened, because the air in there was just too stuffy to breathe for anyone reasonably young and excited about what she or he was doing. At the moment, the result is a mess, an incredible arena for amusement and play... for creative thought... but also occasional blowups (in unfair criticism), and headlong falls into quite existential questions.

Just look at the map, look at the ideals that accompanied the emergence of classical geography in ancient Greece: is that "our" way of knowing the world? That way of distancing, of geometrizing,... is it a women's way of perception and representation?

The history of ideas says it has not been so: Blumenberg tells about the laughter of the Thrakian maid, watching Thales as he fell into the well while his eyes were measuring the skies. Through the philosophical thought of the centuries the story persists, although in many different versions. His thoughts are in the higher spheres; she is the earthy, practical one. This basic distinction carries through almost all later versions, even though she, or more generally the other, changes from the young to the old, from the native to the foreign, from the free to the slave, from one to the many, from the female to the male. But he, Thales, does not change. It is almost inconceivable to see him as female.

And then there was her laughter. Because she did not understand, or because she knew better? Laughing along with her, we never know. We just wonder. Is woman of earth and of home? And what are the merits of ending up in a well with a broken neck? Or, did he, for some strange reason, simply get more publicity?

Imagine Maria Sybilla Merian and her daughter, in 1699, setting sail from Amsterdam to collect caterpillars in Surinam for her scientific investigations on the transformations of butterflies. See them stumbling, see her bleeding legs on her way to catch larvae – to poison and preserve rather than to eat. See the natives wondering, shaking their heads, maybe even laughing. Imagine the comments of those back in Europe. Crazy woman!

Part II: Colombian ones

What do I want to show? Thinking about gender difference is about saying yes, and at the same time questioning it. About learning to differentiate according to situation. The symbolic is there, probably the most ancient cultural ordering there is, creating some of the most striking images of control and dependence today. I have two brief Colombian stories for illustration.

The Laguna de Iguaque is an old Chibcha Indian sanctuary. Following the legend, the goddess Bachue one day emerged with her child to give further birth to the population of the area. Once this was completed they returned to the small mountain lake, disappeared, and then reappeared as large snakes. I do not know too much about the precise meaning of the different symbols – somehow they tell about life and its re-creation. For us it was good ground to think and talk about our legends and descriptions of work and recreation as we were walking through the wet luxuriant forest, and then over the paramo – a form of Andean heath with its characteristic yellow flowers – to climb up to the small sanctuary, helping each other, so that all would reach it. Before, the park ranger had shown us a video of the area and given us geographic explanations, but I guess most of us preferred the pilgrimage up to Bachue's laguna.

Now the second story. In the largest, most luxurious shopping center of Bogotá, where the poor are chased away, and middle class women go window shopping, rather than buying, there was a Christmas contest. The first prize would go to the woman who most resembled a Barbie Doll. This is a Barbie Honkong made, sister of Barbie Venezuela made, or Honkong made as well, a copy of the copy of the copy of the – who knows? American? U.S.American? – original. I borrowed it from my niece. There must be millions of them around worldwide. Barbie Colombia looks just the same, she probably reached her destination on some smuggler's boat. Do you think she is pretty? Does she look like a goddess? Who's goddess? Will she give birth? And what will her children look like? Whoops, here's one, all plastic too! Didn't expect any different, doesn't even look Swiss, didn't drink enough Nestlé chocolate. Universal Miss, doesn't need a place to go diving, won't ever turn into a snake.

Why on earth should Colombian women try to look like Barbie? Who is that good for? We have certain suspicions.

The symbolic is there and it is incredibly powerful. To neglect it is simply stupid for any science that claims to provide explanations about how people live together and use resources. But equally, it is changing, mirroring wider material and immaterial relations. Bachue was probably not so much a woman in our sense, but more simply a birth-giving being, for admiration by anyone who would care for the Indians and their land and their work. Barbie is a plastic image of an ideal modern western woman, made to buy and to imitate everywhere, rather than to admire somewhere. It becomes evident that "Woman" itself is a concept that has been constructed and reconstructed. And now even deconstructed?

Part III: Above, beneath and beyond the symbol

But then, woman is more than a concept. Sometimes there are real bodies to the concept, polluting pure thought. I will never forget the image of the backs of a herd of uniformed women workers set off by the ring of the bell in the flower processing plant, running for home. All young women, running. Turning their back on hundreds of bundles of carnations in buckets filled with preserving solutions and dozens of boxes filled with red roses for cool storage and rapid transportation across the ocean to be sold and resold, bought and re-bought, finally to reach a destination; perhaps to tell her, who is not supposed to leave the cozy home, that she is a privileged, special one, that her work is love work not entangled with the atrocities of the capitalist work place's calculations. Keep still, flowers are getting affordable, for anyone – here.

The examples I have drawn together here may seem to be rather disparate, and I guess to some extent they are. But still, why should the Appenzell woman, Thales' maid, Maria Sibylla Merian and her daughter, Bachue and the Colombian student, Barbie and the mother who buys her, the flower worker and her (female) manager, the flower store girl and the house wife, and maybe even a human geographer come together for a business lunch?

The Calanca valley women could host them. They remind us of a time not more than 50 years ago, when they were the center of the family enterprise, producing and voting, at least at the family kitchen table. Statistics show them vanishing into faceless housewives, without a profession, without income, without much to say, their knowledge, cared for and respected over the centuries, suddenly depreciated. Convening, the women will show each other the tired bodies from hard farm labor; broken bodies from the endless diets to reach out to the plastic ideal; poisoned bodies from the fungicides, herbicides, pesticides and preserving chemicals to keep the colors fresh, from antidepressive drugs and too much alcohol. They will ask Maria Sybilla how it was to set sail, and Bachue how she could keep giving birth and they will laugh with the maid. They might go to the places where 300 years ago witches were burned for their knowledge and their desire to dance. And they will get together to start taking charge, changing cultural orders to protect their bodies and their lives.

A few last remarks. I do not think the discrimination I have been illustrating is exclusive to women. But women's bodies provide for one of the most striking, if not the most striking, target for symbolic-economic exploitation. As I have sugested, I suspect matters to get worse rather than better. Behind a veil of official 'equal rights' – based on a questionable tradition of ideals anyways – exploitation is transfered to more subtle levels of communication, and then, not so subtly to other areas of the globe.

This should concern geography for at least two reasons. One, because spatial confinement is instrumental in shaping orders for many women. Second, because thinking about women, their forms of knowledge, their conceptions of time and mobility, is deeply subversive to most forms of geographic description. It would have been very improbable for Columbus to have been a woman, even though, as the story of Maria Merian suggests, it cannot be excluded all together. But then, would the notes in her logbook have been the same as his and his followers'? To think about it is to dream and to speculate. Journals of woman anthropologists and personal experience suggest a chance for different access and other modes of communication. The base is a concept itself in motion, the direction is subversive and constructive, and so full of contradictions. We have to use the language and the institutions, we have to take seriously and care for what we plan to subvert, we have to float on her rippling laughter...

Reference

Blumenberg H, 1987 *Das Lachen der Thrakerin* (Suhrkamp, Frankfurt am Main)

(RE)CONSTRUCTIVELY RE-PRESENTING THE PRESENT, IMAGE-INING THE CONTEMPORARY WORLD, RESONATING WITH THE CONDITION(ING)S OF HYPERMODERNITY

by Allan Pred

"Method of this work: literary montage. I have nothing to say, only to show."
Walter Benjamin (1982, p.574) as quoted in Susan Buck-Morss (1989, p.73)

* * * * * * *

"What we [as cosmopolitan intellectuals] share as a condition of existence ... is a specificity of historical experience and place, however complex and contestable they might be, and a worldwide macro-interdependency encompassing any local particularity. Whether we like it or not, we are all in this situation."
Paul Rabinow (1986, p.258)

* * * * * * *

In our writing,
how may we as intellectuals,
        as human geographers,
        as corpo-real beings,
        as knowing, thinking and feeling subjects,
        as self-reflexive women and men,
make sense of the world
    for ourselves and for others;
at one and the same time make the here and now,
    and its then and there antecedents,
intelligible,
    while still giving artful, art-filled play

to our imag(e)inations?
How may we (re)constructively re-present the present,
creatively produce on-the-page images
of our mental images and reflective reworkings
    of the contemporary world(s)
        in which our everyday lives are interwoven,
        in which our observations and hearings are enmeshed,
        from which our categories and metaphors are derived?

How may we capture those sounds
    which resonate with the circumstances of hypermodernity,
        with the very condition(ing)s of our lives
            and our writings?

* * * * * * *

Have I
in the phrasing of the above questions,
in the selection of words, stops and silences,
in the calculated deployment of indentations, hyphens and parentheses,
already provided a signpost,
        an en route set of indicators,
        an abbreviated inventory of possible destinations,
already suggested an answer
        or two, three, four, ...
already demonstrated that-
    like it or not-
the p(r)o(s)etics of one's textual strategy
are the politics of one's textual strategy?

* * * * * * *

"The effect of technology on both work and leisure in the modern metropolis has been to shatter experience into fragments."
                              Susan Buck-Morss (1989, p.23)

* * * * * * *

Upon situated reflection . . . .

There is no taking issue
with the denial of a unitary human history,
    of a single history of "man,"
    of an unilinear, uninterrupted story of progress,
    of a monolithic Euro-centric history,
    of history with a capital H.

There is no taking issue
with the rejection of metanarratives,
    of narratives which make all other narratives subordinate,
        which make claims to the totalistic,
            to the completely overarching,
            to the all encompassing.

For any one place as well as the world at large, for the present moment as well as any given period of the past, there cannot be one grand history, one grand human geography, whose telling only awaits an appropriate metanarrative. Through their engagement in a multitude of situated practices, through their participation in a multitude of juxtaposed power relations, people make a multitude of histories and construct a multitude of human geographies.

If the appropriateness of metanarratives is readily cast aside, the appropriateness of MEGAnarratives- of narratives which encompass large pieces of all that is ever-becoming- is not so easily denied in a world in which the practices and power relations of patriarchy, capitalism, racism and bureaucratic rationality are extremely widespread, if not all pervasive.

The rejection of metanarratives without any recognition of meganarratives merely "allow[s] those with power to counter the increasingly insistent challenge from those at the margins." [1]

* * * * * * *

Whatever our scale of reference, the contemporary world (or any past world) is neither a completely integrated totality, nor a chaotic pastiche, a jumble of atomistic, unrelated fragments.

The world of individuals and the world of collectivities,
the contemporary social world writ small
    and the contemporary social world writ large,
cannot be anything but a totality of fragments,
    a totality of corpo-really, structurally and symbolically
        interconnected fragments,
cannot be anything but an assemblage
    of physically and socially encountered fragments,
        none of which stands meaninglessly on its own,
        each of which meaningfully touches upon others,
        most of which are associated with power structures,
        all of which are not
            bound up in a single structure of power and meaning.

This is so
as human beings are inescapably embodied beings,
as they are always literally in touch
    with (transformed and culturally mediated) nature,
    with the material and the concrete,
as they cannot but trace an uninterrupted path through space and time
    from the moment of their birth to the moment of their death,
as their everyday lives and their entire biographies
    unavoidably course through situated practices,
        through institutionally embedded practices,
whose associated power relations are of varying geographic extent,

---

[1] *McDowell (1992, p.65). McDowell is addressing the postmodernist stance on metanarratives, rather than the question of what are here termed meganarratives. Her position echoes that of Haraway, Hartsock, Spivak and other key feminist theorists.*

whose forms of knowledge, language and meaning
become differently superimposed,
differently shared.

* * * * * * *

"The Passagen-Werk *suggests that it makes no sense to divide the era of capitalism into formalist 'modernism' and historically eclectic 'post-modernism,' as those tendencies have been there from the start of industrial culture. The paradoxical dynamics of novelty and repetition simply repeat themselves anew.*

Modernism and postmodernism are not chronological eras, but political positions in the century-long struggle between art and technology. If modernism expresses utopian longing by anticipating the reconciliation of social function and aesthetic form, postmodernism acknowledges their nonidentity and keeps fantasies alive. Each position thus represents a partial truth; each will recur 'anew' so long as the contradictions of commodity society are not overcome."

Susan Buck-Morss (1989, p.359)

* * * * * * *

Neither the demise of various "high modernisms,"
nor the existence of a "postmodern" architectural style,
    of a by now trite register of pastiche, eclectical historical borrowing
        and "double codings,"
nor the existence of a "postmodern" (anti)aesthetic within the arts,
nor the existence of a (sometimes incompatible) set
    of language-centered "postmodern" academic discourses,
is to be conflated with a "postmodern" world of everyday life,
is to be equated with a "postmodern" epoch,
is to be confused with a lived and experienced "postmodern" condition.

The day-to-day and minute-to-minute
    worlds in which we live

are perhaps post- "high modern,"
but difficult to defend as *post*modern;
for,
any placing of the ear to the ground
    of past times and places
would aurally reveal that we are not literally beyond the modern.

The practices and experiences of everyday life during the modernity of early industrial capitalisms were characterized in geographically specific ways by encounters
with the transitory and the apparently fragmented,
with an incessant spectacle of the new,
with repeated material evidence of creative destruction,
with relentlessly expanding commodification,
with fleeting forms of consumption
    and a dreamworld of commodity fetishism,
with constant changes in employment opportunities and circumstances,
with ephemeral and disjointed social contacts,
with the persistent spread of bureaucratic rationality
    and its iron-cage rules,
with powerful new technologies and new technologies of power.

In short,
these were encounters
with plural complexities and
with shockingly new meanings
    that dislocated and displaced,
    that confirmed rupture,
    that called the meanings
        of locally preexisting practices and social relations
            into question,
    and thereby called individual and collective identities
        into question.

This being the case,
then the everyday life and experiences of the here and now,

of the 1990s in specific places,
however clearly distinctive they may be,
however radically altered they may have become
    by post-Fordist,
        post-Colonial or
        post-Cold War circumstances,
are best characterized as modernity magnified,
as modernity accentuated and sped up,
as hypermodern,
not postmodern.

* * * * * * *

If a modernism is an intellectual or artistic reworking or rejection
    of the experiences of modernity,
then any self-declared postmodernism
    any discursive claim that everything turns on language
        (which denies the mutual embeddedness
            of language, situated practices and power relations
                within one another),
    any artistic avowal of pastiche and the fragmented
        ("which sees the jumbling of elements as all there is,")[2]
is but another modernism,
or, more accurately,
a hypermodernism.[3]

* * * * * * *

If there is an extensive "crisis of representation,"
    a failure of the link between signifier and signified
        to remain fixed or stable,
it is, as much as anything,
a hypermodern

---

2 Rabinow (1986, p.249), rephrasing Jameson (1983). Also note Jameson (1991).
3 It is characteristic of the conditions of hypermodernity that some people have already begun to refer to "postmodernism" in the past tense (Rosenthal, 1992).

rather than a postmodern crisis.

If there is a "crisis of representation"
within academic and literary worlds,
    a situation where the *only* referent is other sentences,
        other texts,
        other printed discourses,
it emerges in some measure from the asymmetries
    between deeply sedimented,
        largely unexamined and
        unreflectingly reproduced representational practices,
    or, practices that are norm-ally unilinear, neatly sequenced
        (even when addressing simultaneous diversity),
    and the condition(ing)s of hypermodernity
    experienced outside those worlds.

If there is a "crisis of representation,"
    a refusal of central meanings to stand still,
    a breakdown of identities,
it to a considerable extent derives
from the repeated realignment and revision
    of the everyday practices and power relations
    in which language and meaning are embedded,
from multiply recurring experiences of incongruity and rupture,
from an accelerated tendency for everyday practices
    to be engineered or controlled by nonlocal agents
        of capital or the State,
from a consequently accelerated tendency
    for the truth of experience
    to no longer coincide with the place in which it takes place.[4]

* * * * * * *

[4] This final phrase is a rewording of Jameson (1988, p.35). As Gregory (1991, p.17) notes, by the onset of the twentieth century "such a disassociation between ... structured and lived experience had been transcoded into a radically new relation between space and place." Also note Gregory (1993).

Whatever else you or I may choose to say about the matter,
at some level,
everything we write,
including our efforts to (re)constructively re-present the present,
        to image(-ine) on paper the contemporary world,
involves a reworking of our situated experiences,
and, thereby,
it resonates with particular condition(ing)s of hypermodernity.

* * * * * * *

However much we exert ourselves,
however much we deny it,
there is no abstracting from
    (a multiplicity of differentiating)
power relations.

* * * * * * *

"*[The Condition of Postmodernity] was written ... from a relatively privileged position within the belly of the beast that is capitalism. It was written with the primary intention of giving the beast a belly-ache. But it was also written to try and remind many who seem to have forgotten or mislaid the sense of it, that this particular situatedness is both important and revealing. For this reason, it did indeed emphasize the situatedness of postmodernism within the belly of the capitalist beast.*"

"*... a cogent framework (though not the whole story) for explanation of what postmodernism is all about.*"

                      David Harvey *(1992, pp.304, 311)*

* * * * * * *

[In his One Way Street *(Einbahnstrasse) and the notes and*

*drafts for his Arcades Project (*Das Passagen-Werk*),*[5] *in his efforts to critically re-present and de-myth-ologize the circulation of commodities] Benjamin effectively 'spatialised' time, supplanting the narrative encoding of history through a textual practice that disrupted the historiographic chain in which moments are clipped together like magnets. In practice this required him to reclaim the debris of history from the matrix of [linear, progressive] systematicity in which historiography had embedded it: to blast the fragments from their all-too-familiar, taken-for-granted and, as Benjamin would insist, their* mythical *context and place them in a new, radically heterogeneous setting in which their integrities would not be fused into one. This practice of montage was derived from the surrealists, of course, who used it to dislocate the boundaries between art and life."*

Derek Gregory (1991, p.26)[6]

"*For Benjamin, the technique of montage had 'special, perhaps even total rights' as a progressive form because it 'interrupts the context into which it is inserted' and thus 'counteracts illusion.'*"

"*When Benjamin praised montage as progressive because it 'interrupts the context into which it is inserted,' he was referring to its destructive critical dimension ... . But the task of the Arcades project was to implement as well the constructive dimension of the montage, as the only form in which modern philosophy could be erected.*"

"*[I]f Benjamin threw the traditional language of metaphysics*

---

5 Benjamin (1979) and (1982).

6 As a conscious art form, montage had its apparent origins in the photomontages of Georg Grosz, Hannah Höch, other Berlin Dadaists, and especially John Heartfield, who, during the late twenties and thirties, brought this mode of political collage "to a pitch of polemical ferocity that no artist has since equalled" (Hughes, 1991, p.73). Their images "directly cut from the 'reckless everyday psyche' of the press, stuck next to and on top of one another in ways that resembled the laps and dissolves of film editing, ... could combine the grip of a dream with the documentary 'truth' of photography" (Hughes, 1991, p71). Note Buck-Morss (1989, pp.60-64) on the parallels between Heartfield's work during the thirties and that of Benjamin. Also see Bürger (1984, p.66 ff) on Benjamin, avant-garde art and allegory.

into the junkroom, it was to rescue the metaphysical experience of the objective world, not to see philosophy dissolve into the play of language itself."

Susan Buck-Morss (1989, pp.67, 77, 223)

* * * * * * *

Not a matter of either/or, but of both/and...

*"[The idea] is formulated in one place, of the work [*The Arcades Project*] as pure 'montage,' that is created from a juxtaposition of quotation so that the theory springs out of it without having to be inserted as interpretation."*

"In place of mediating theory, the form of commentary was to have appeared which he defined as interpretation out of the particulars. ... The quotations are instead the material that Benjamin's representation [interpretation and commentary] was to employ."

Theodor Adorno (1949)[7]

* * * * * * *

Benjamin's "montage" is a highly suggestive point of departure.
A source of intellectual inspiration.
Not a work of art to be mechanically reproduced.

Benjamin's writing resonated with the condition(ing)s of modernity
    in Berlin during his childhood,
    in Berlin and Paris during the twenties and thirties.
Our writings resonate with the condition(ing)s of hypermodernity
    in our particular worlds during the nineties.

---

7 Theodor Adorno in a letter to Max Horkheimer (May, 1949) and Rolf Tiedemann, editor of the Passagen-Werk, *as quoted in* Susan Buck-Morss (1989, pp.73-74)

Benjamin did not make it over the mountains with his baggage.[8]
We are still carrying ours.
Time to unpack!

* * * * * * *

In attempting to (re)constructively re-present the present
        and its modern antecedents
through the medium of montage,
through the juxtaposing of verbal and visual fragments,
through the juxtaposing of quotations,
    newspaper reports,
    anecdotes,
    jokes,
    other ethnographic evidence of symbolic discontent,
    aphorisms, and
    more conventional summary statements and notes,
with photographs, art reproductions and cartoons,
one may attempt to art-iculate
as well as resonate
at several levels at once.[9]

Through assembling (choice) bits
    and (otherwise neglected or discarded) scraps,
through the cut-and-paste reconstructions of montage,
one may bring alive,
open the text to multiple ways of knowing
    and multiple sets of meaning,
allow multiple voices to be heard,
    to speak to (or past) each other

---

8 *Fleeing Paris in 1940 after it fell to Hitler's troops, Benjamin picked up an U.S. visa in Marseilles and eventually crossed into Spain with some fellow exiles at Port Bou. Confronted by a local official who threatened (for blackmail purposes) to return them in the morning to France and the Gestapo, he took an overdose of morphine. Had he waited until the following day, he actually would have been permitted to proceed to Lisbon.*
9 *For initial, groping efforts along these lines see Pred (1991, 1992, 1993).*

as well as to the contexts from which they emerge
and to which they contribute.

Through deliberately deploying the devices of montage,
one may, simultaneously,
reveal what is most central to the place and time in question,
    to the operative question,
by confronting the ordinary with the extraordinary,
    the commonplace with the out-of-place,
    the (would-be) hegemonic with the counterhegemonic,
    the ruling with the unruly,
    the power wielders with the subjects of power,
    the margin definers with the marginalized,
    the boundary drawers with the out-of-bounds,
    the norm makers with the "abnormal,"
    the dominating with the dominated.

Through the combinatory possibilities of montage,
one may uncover what is otherwise covered over,
and, simultaneously,
bring into significant conjuncture
    what otherwise would appear unrelated,
blast into isolated disjuncture
    what would otherwise would be buried with insignificance,
over and over again
focusing on tiny, seemingly inconsequential details,
    on fragments of no apparent significance,
so as to project the largest possible picture,
so as to provide an intelligible account-
    an array of truthful knowledges-
which is as partial as possible.

Through the calculated arrangements of montage,
one may present- from re-presented particulars-
    a particular interpretation,
and, simultaneously,

allow theory and theoretical position to speak for themselves,
    to emerge from the spatial (juxta)positions of the text,
        from the silent spaces
        which force discordant fragments
            to whisper and SHOUT at each other in polylogue.

Through the de-signing and re-signing designs of montage,
one may confront the reader
    with the possibility of seeing and hearing
        what she would otherwise neither see, nor hear,
    with the possibility of making associations,
        that otherwise would go unmade,
by subtly demanding that the meaning of each fragment
    be enhanced and shifted repeatedly
        as a consequence of preceding-fragment echoes
            and subsequent-fragment contents.

In the end,
through all of these simultaneous strivings,
through the maneuvered configurations of montage,
through the intercutting of a set of (geographical hi)stories,
through a strategy of radical heterogeneity,
through (c)rudely juxtaposing the incompatible and contradictory,
one may attempt to bring component fragments into mutual illumination,
    and thereby startle.

One may, in other words,
attempt to illuminate
    by way of shock,
        by way of a stunning constellation,
attempt to jolt out of position
        by suggesting a totality of fragments,
without insisting upon a closure
    that does not exist.

In the process,

    explicitly and implicity,
raising as many questions
as are answered.

All the while
showing as much about oneself
    as about anything else,
showing as much about one's place in a hypermodern world,
    as about the in-place practices and power relations
        of the hypermodern world itself.

                * * * * * * *

    "There is a contradiction between creativity and socialization. Just as the overriding aim of the former is the creation of the new, so the overriding aim of the latter is the preservation of the old."
                                    Gunnar Olsson (1991, p.28)

Montage is transgression
    of the (hyper)modern condition(ing)s
    out of which it is created.
In demanding new associations,
    new connections that transcend taken-for-granted meanings,
it also demands transgressions
on the part of those who read it.

The well socialized do not comply with transgressive demands.
The creative comply in their own way.

                * * * * * * *

    "Benjamin's heteroclite constellation seems to mine the same historico-geographical vein [as Foucault's archeology]: in both cases 'archeology' is not so much an excavation, bringing buried or hidden objects to the surface, as a way of showing the particular- anonymous, dispersed- practices and the particular-

differentiated, hierarchized- spaces through which particular societies make particular things visible."

Derek Gregory (1991, p.36)

* * * * * * *

"Benjamin had, indeed, not made things easy on himself."

Susan Buck-Morss (1989, p.23)

References

Benjamin W, 1979 *One Way Street and other writings.* (New Left Books, London)

Benjamin W, 1982 *Gesammelte Schriften*, vol. 5, *Das Passagen- Werk* Ed R Tiedemann (Suhrkamp Verlag, Frankfurt am Main)

Buck-Morss S, 1989 *The Dialetics of Seeing: Walter Benjamin and the Arcades Project.* (The MIT Press, Cambridge, Mass.)

Bürger P, 1984 *Theory of the Avant-Garde.* (University of Minneapolis Press, Minneapolis)

Gregory D, 1991 "Interventions in the Historical Geography of Modernity: Social Theory, Spatiality and the Politics of Representation," *Geografiska Annaler, 73B*, pp. 17-44

Gregory D, 1993 *Geographical Imaginations* (Basil Blackwell, Oxford).

Harvey D, 1989, *The Condition of Postmodernity- An Enquiry into the Origins of Culture Change* (Basil Blackwell, Oxford)

Harvey D, 1992, "Postmodern Morality Plays," *Antipode, 24*, pp. 300-326

Hughes R, 1991 *The Shock of the New*, revised edition. (Alfred A. Knopf, New York)

Jameson F, 1983, "Postmodernism and Consumer Society," in *The Anti-Aesthetic: Essays on Postmodern Culture.* Ed H Foster (Bay Press, Port Townsend,Wash.) pp. 111-125

Jameson F, 1988, "Cognitive Mapping," in *Marxism and the Interpretation of Culture.* Ed C Nelson and L Grossberg, (University of Illinois Press, Urbana) pp. 347-360

Jameson F, 1991 *Postmodernism, or, The Cultural Logic of Late Capitalism.* (Duke University Press, Durham, N.C.)

McDowell L, 1992, "Multiple Voices: Speaking from Inside and Outside 'the Project,'" *Antipode, 24*, pp. 56-72

Olsson G, 1991 *Lines of Power/Limits of Language.* (University of Minnesota Press, Minneapolis)

Pred A, 1991 "Spectacular Articulations of Modernity: The Stockholm Exhibition of 1897," *Geografiska Annaler, 73B*, pp. 45-84

Pred A, 1992, "Pure and Simple Lines, Future Lines of Vision: The Stockholm Exhibition of 1930," *Nordisk Samhällsgeografisk Tidskrift, 15*, pp. 3-61

Pred A, 1993, "Where in the World Am I, Are We? Who in the World Am I, Are We?: The Glob(e)alization of Stockholm, Sweden." To appear (along with Pred 1991, 1992) in *Swedish Modern: Spectacular Spaces of Consumption and Hegemonic Discourses; or, A Montage of the Present*, forthcoming.

Rabinow P, 1986, "Representations Are Social Facts: Modernity and Post-Modernity in Anthropology," in *Writing Culture: The Poetics and Politics of Ethnography.* Eds J Clifford and G E Marcus (University of California Press, Berkeley), pp. 234-261

Rosenthal M, 1992, "What Was Postmodernism?," *Socialist Review, 22*, no. 3, pp. 83-105

GLOBAL AND LOCAL GEO-GRAPHIES

by Giuseppe Dematteis

Two paths

Since ancient times, geographers have always followed two paths: one is that of seeking visible forms capable of representing given meanings and values, the other that of suggesting meanings and values latent in evident forms. With some schematization one can say that the first path corresponds to the search for a signifier to express a signified, whereas the second corresponds to the search for one or more of the possible signifieds of a signifier. In the first case, we are close to the Saussurian signified/signifier relationship, and therefore to the problems of persuasion and scientific certainties. In the second, we are nearer to the Lacanian relationship of signifier/signified and to the problems of creativity and hermeneutics.

In geography, the signifier forms refer to that which is observable of the Earth's surface: territorial objects such as mountains, rivers, cities, borders and the relationships between them (positions, distances, configurations, topology etc.). The evidence of the latter derives from the unwitting application of a certain spatial syntax which in modern western culture is Euclidean. As I have maintained elsewhere (Dematteis 1985a,1987), there is more to geography than the representation of the Earth's surface in order to gain information about the material formation of the environment in which we live. While it performs this practical function, it also uses the same representations as the geo-graphies of the world, or in other words, as a system of metonymes and metaphors which connect the "evident" order of things to a certain socio-poltical one: both to the existing order (normal geo-graphies, prevalently metonymic) and to a possible one (innovative geo-graphies, prevalently metaphoric).[1] If one

---

[1] Obviously, also in normal geographies, an implicit scheme can be recognized, if none other than that of reproducing and expanding the order that they represent.

may speak of a geographic language, it should not be identified, as in "normal"sciences, with a specialized, lexical, syntactical structure tending towards rigorous definition. Geographers have always used common language, taking advantage of its ambiguity and plasticity to create, as has been said, a systematic translation of signifieds from the field of physical forms to that of relationships between actors; this is the only code that constitutes the language of geography, an open code which can be reconstructed afterwards.[2]

Ambivalent representations are derived from this which give rise to necessities and certainties and, at the same time, reveal even unwittingly, new signifieds and suggest latent matrices of meanings (Dematteis 1985b). In this way, each geography oscillates between the prescriptive determinism of metonymies and the free creativity of metaphors. P. Vidal de la Blache (1903) thus affirmed that geography is "the science of places and not of man" but he later had to recognize that a country is a "medallion which can be coined according to the effigy of a people". Before him, A. von Humboldt trod the same path in the opposite direction: he started out from the artistic-literary category of landscape, developing it into a vehicle of new signifieds capable of introducing him into the scientific study of the natural order of the Earth (Farinelli 1981).

Today, the real problem of geography would seem to be that of the reversibility of the two above mentioned paths. It is not sufficient to deconstruct geo-graphies by unveiling their hidden matrices and it would be naive to believe that with this one can "surpass" the geographic representations as forms limited to the superficial appearance of reality and therefore subject to ideological manipulation.[3] If this is so, it certainly does not apply only to geography; the very critical reflective discourse is based upon categories of which the

---

[2] *The attempts of neo-positivist inspiration at reducing geography to a "normal" science have not modified its structure: they have merely imported exogenous languages inside the discipline, with the main positive result of demonstrating the limits of any banally referential concept of geography (Harvey 1969, Olsson 1980).*

[3] *Something of this kind would suggest a reading of Farinelli's Geneva lectures (1989), but I believe that their transcription has simplified the author's thoughts, who in the preface confesses, "Je n'ai ni ecrit, ni peut être dit les paroles qui suivent".*

original matrices (often geo-graphic) have been largely forgotten. What appears interesting in geography is actually the fact that it offers the opportunity of deconstructive and constructive critical and creative paths. It presupposes a meta-geography (a geography capable of self-description), which means that one can turn back upon these paths at any given time. And this is what will be done in the following pages as far as local and global geo-graphies are concerned.

Global/local

The global/local relationship in geography takes on the literal form of a relationship between that which concerns the entire globe and that which applies to individual regions or places. The field of possible interpretations of such a relationship varies, however, according to whether we consider global/local as a prevalently metonymic expression or essentially metaphoric. In the first case, the best means of representation (and it has been the dominant one since the 18th century) is the metric areal one (Euclid-Cartesian) where by global we mean the entire Earth's surface, and by local a part of it in the physical sense. In the second case, however, instead of referring to a physical entity we refer to the interaction between actors: global is the *network* of such interactions, local is the *nodes* of the network i.e. individual actors or, more often, local systems of actors. In this case, the spatial operator used is not metric but topological, even if it is easily translatable into lines and points and can therefore be represented on a geographical map.

While in an areal representation space is considered as an empirical entity whose general properties (continuity, homogeneousness etc.) and local ecological ones intervene in the phenomena represented, (be they natural or socio-historical), in networked representations, space becomes a simple means of description.

Some of the key words in contemporary geography are derived from the combination of the global/local and the areal/networked pairs.

Representations	Structures, processes	
areal	TERRITORY	PLACE REGION
networked	NETWORKS	CENTRE NODE

The reversibility of the geo-graphies constructed upon these categories implies a response to the question: "What differences in meaning derive from representing the global as a continuous territory or rather as a network, and the local as a portion of a territory or rather as a node in a network?"
Here are some fundamental contradictions in meaning contained in the above alternative:

AREAL (territory, places, regions)	NETWORKED (networks, nodes, centres)
Metonymies of geographical distance: similar because near, different because far	metaphoric distances: that which is similar is near, that which is different is far
Negative central-peripheral gradients	a criss-cross of local networks with both "central" and "peripheral" features ("mosaic")
Metric cartography	symbolic cartography, metacartography (?)
Stable, rooted	changeable, mobile
"Ordnung and Ortnung" (Schmitt 1974)	flows
Land ownership, territorial dominance, borders	control of flows; multilocation
Panopticon	television, videotel
Hierarchy of places and regions (nesting)	hierarchy of networks
Conservation, security	instability, destructive innovation (Schumpeter)
Territorialization (Raffestin 1984)	de-territorialization and re-territorialization (Raffestin 1984)
Specificity, dialects	homologation, universal languages
Certainties, necessity	ambiguity, chance, possibility

In areal representations, the global is made up of "horizontal" relations in which relationships between actors are reduced to relations between places, while the local is a combination of "vertical" relationships which make the agency of each actor dependent on the stable characteristics (natural and historical) of the places they occupy.

In areal representations, conflicts are purely territorial and are normally seen as anomalies, in that the territory tends towards a state of equilibrium derived from global balancing.

Networked representations, however, are exclusively "horizontal" but not determining: they represent relationships between actors in a state of constant change which have unpredictable outcomes. In these types of geo-graphies, the global level does not necessarily determine the local one. As we shall see later on, the nodes can be considered as entities autonomous to the network, and the observer may shift position and adopt contemporaneously both a global and local point of view, as if they were complementary, even if (or actually because) this implies accepting contradictions at a logical level and conflicts at a practical one.

The limits of areal representations are determinism, static nature and in short, treating social relationships and processes as similar to mechanistic relationships between things. The projects, being "servile translations" of this "objective" reality, are reduced to the limited horizons of socio-territorial engineering (Olsson 1980 chapter14, and 1991b).

The limit of networked interpretations is indeterminateness, the atomistic fragmentation of points of view at the node level, the interconnection of nodes to unconstrained networks resulting in an emptying of meanings: duration, stability and memory thus disappear; the present invades the field of representation, excluding the past and resulting also in a loss of any sense of the future.

If areal representations lend themselves to legitimizing ad reproducing the existing order, whatever it may be, networked ones can be seen to legitimize the fatality of change, whatever direction it may take. But the alternative between these two geo-graphies, those of the photocopy and those of the coup de dès, is never radical because, as mentioned previously, they are simply the two extreme poles between which the field of geographical representations extends.

Four geo-graphies

If we forget that to observe, to describe and to represent are *actions* based upon implicit *choices* connected to the world of intentions, then geography may appear as an innocent science, as W.Bunge (1966) optimistically saw it, at the times of the "quantitative revolution".

The unaware or passive geographer neither knows nor wonders why he observes the world from a certain point of view or why he describes it according to certain rules. In this way, he is convinced of being objective and of constructing true representations, but being unable to describe his own descriptions, he cannot prove it. Neither can he say whether the properties of the objects which he describes belong to them or to the modality of the description or to the projects implicit therein. His justification is the old adage, "The myth is not mine, I received it from my mother" (Euripedes, line 488).

The conscious or active geographer, on the other hand, assumes personal responsibility for the choices implicit in his observation processes and descriptions and can therefore justify and, if necessary, modify these in the course of discursive interaction.

The geographer, whether passive or active, can also place his observation point inside or outside the object considered; using our pair in a very abstract manner it is equivalent to saying that he can assume both a local and a global vision. The active geographer will thus be able to move around between several local and global points of view, whereas if the passive geographer assumes an internal point of view (local) when considering a given territorial context, it cannot become external and vice versa.

Combining these two pairs we circumscribe the fields of four ab stract geo-graphies.[4]

	EXTERNAL POINT OF VIEW (global)	INTERNAL POINT OF VIEW (local)
PASSIVE OBSERVER	1 modern geo-graphies	3 pre-modern geo-graphies
ACTIVE OBSERVER	2 hyper-modern geo-graphies	4 the geo-graphies of complexity

• *Modern* geo-graphies are still dominant. They have the characteristics of areal representation. The local is seen as part of the global, that is as a portion of the Earth's surface. But this global is none other than a "inflated local" (Serres 1980, p. 75): hence the world seen through the eyes of Western European culture of the 16th century (Toulmin 1990, Derrida 1991) and then, as a consequence, transformed.

• *Pre-modern* geo-graphies are essentially local visions which the (passive) observer identifies with the global without claiming to "inflate it". On the contrary, here quite the opposite operation occurs. The "horizontal" relationships tend to disappear and all sense of representation tends to be attributed to "vertical" relationships and to connections to certain roots. It is the global which "collapses" onto the local; the area tends towards the point, or the latest manifestation of the word before silence (Kandinsky 1928, quoted in Olsson 1991).

• *Hypermodern* geo-graphies,[5] in renouncing the fixedness of the

---

4 *I got the idea for this classification from the proposal put forward by A. Lanzani (short presentation at the Seminar on Landscape planning, Regione Autonoma Valle d'Aosta, Saint-Vincent, AO, January 1991) which illustrates the different approaches to landscape planning by creating intersections between the pairs formed by active/passive planning and active/passive local society.*

5 *According to some authors (Harvey 1989, Soja 1989, Gregory 1989) these geo-graphies could be called post-modern. For reasons that I shall give below, this term would be better suited to the type 5 geo-graphy. However, so as not to create confusion or pose false problems I shall not insist upon this.*

observation point, become a sort of kaleidoscope in which the observer shifts himself continually. These therefore have the previously mentioned characteristics of mobility, relativity and indeterminateness of networked representations. They tend to represent the world as a network of purely "horizontal" relationships, free of any "vertical" territorial rooting, which multiply their connections beyond all constraints of significance and sense to the point of producing pure and simple noise.

It is more difficult to speak of the fourth type of geo-graphies. If *pre-modern* geo-graphies tend towards silence, as a local meaning in its pure state; if the *hypermodern* geo-graphies tend towards noise as global signifier free of significance; if the intermediate *modern* phase appears to be a local which dilates and encompasses all others, then the fourth type should symmetrically represent the global which returns to consisting of a plurality of "locals" as its active, autonomous and necessary components, with distinct properties and languages, not reducible to those of the global system, yet maintaining the possiblity of connecting general signifiers to different local signifieds and, at the same time, of connecting the latter to each other to the point where the global is represented as a network of locals.

These geo-graphies can therefore be termed ones of *complexity*. What distinguishes them from others is the fact that the observer is included in the observation and the visible maps of this geography cannot be traced unless the invisible maps (Olsson 1991c) which describe the modalities of description are first explored.

Global/local as metaphors for social relationships

The issue of the transformations of the capitalist system is implicit in the previous classifications. *Pre-modern* geographies can be made to correspond to extreme pre-capitalist situations in which the local tends to represent particular utility values in the absence of exchanges based upon general equivalents. *Modern* ones describe intermediate situations in which certain values, orginally local, are imposed as global values. But this "inflated" local maintains the original territorial forms of control (precapitalist) and the connected areal, spatial logics: rooting, territory and state borders, territorial conquest, the control of their position in space according to the Panopticon model (Foucault 1975).

It is known, furthermore, that during this century the direct control of physical space has shown itself to be ever less efficient and feasible, while ever more importance is given to the control of the economy, society and culture through the control of so-called "immaterial" flows, in particular, those of financial capital, of strategic information and of the media (Castells 1989, Goddard 1990, Pred 1990). Since these flows are organized in global networks, the geography of the most advanced social forms of modern society tends to surpass the representations of time and space typical of classic modernity (Harvey 1989).

In particular, the acceleration of change and the constant restructuring imposed by innovative competition show themselves to be incompatible with an ideology of territorial rooting. Furthermore, the cosmopolitanization of cultural exchanges and political interactions, the formation of transnational company networks, the interdepedence of places without the restrictions of geographic distance, thanks to the development of telecommunications and computer science, the consequent processes of flexible accumulation (Harvey 1989), make it impractical to operate controls based upon a fixed physical-spatial order.

From the Panopticon, in which central power is able to control all actors after having fixed each in a precise location, one passes to television (or to videotel, to data banks etc.) in which the location of subjects is unimportant, so long as they are inserted within a network, so that they are controllable by regulating the flows which traverse them.

Everything thus tends to take on a global network pattern and to group into nodes that can link up in various ways without constraints or without necessarily being related to particular places, without references to utility values or to local languages which cannot be totally resolved in exchange values and in universal languages (Raffestin 1981).

Such networked geography is *hypermodern* because it manages better to represent the most evolved stages and, perhaps, the very essence of capitalism and the market as a system of free "horizontal" relationships.

In particular, network systems demonstrate the capacity to surpass and, at the same time, to take over and use what remains of previous areas of control (territorial dominion, land ownership Fordism, socialist planning etc.)

All this, however, is not free of contradictions. These are particularly evident precisely where the nodes of the global networks converge and thicken, i.e. in big cities. What gives global cohesion to this apparently heterogenous group of actors belonging to different organizations and "horizontal" relationships? Why is it that they continue to exist and even establish themselves as autonomous international actors instead of breaking up into different pieces of the global networks which cross them? The only answer to this would seem to be that global networks function by drawing upon environmental conditions and specific infrastructures that present themselves only in given territorial situations. In particular, big cities offer "environmental" externalities derived from the exceptional historical accumulation of cultural resources, fixed social capital and from the intensity of social interaction (Castells 1989, Camagni 1991). Therefore these attract, concentrate and tie together in stable spatial structures the nodes of global networks. The latter should be considered as actors which, beyond the possible functional links with the networks to which they belong, are however obliged to interact on a local basis: they give rise to competitive/cooperative relationships for the use and reproduction of the local environment as a source of strategic externalities (Dematteis 1991).

If this is so, then not only are global networks constituted by "horizontal" relationships between nodes, but are also structures of exchange and communication fed by autonomously organized territorial systems of great stability, in which the specific local values are continally being elaborated and transformed into universal values and circulated within global networks.

Geo-graphies of complexity: possibilities and limits

Hypermodern geographies which reduce everything to "horizontal" relationships and to mobile combinations of fragments, do not appear to be the most appropriate for describing the above mentioned situations. More suited are the geo-graphies that are of sufficient complexity to enable the observer both to assume a global point of view and to take up a position within the various local systems in order to represent their specific values, the autonomous organizing processes capable of transforming them into global values and hence the links between "horizontal" and "vertical" relationships, without ever getting to the point of eliminating the contradictions of the bar which de Saussure placed between signifier and signified (Olsson 1991a, 1991c).

It remains to be seen whether this type of geography is practicable at epistemological and practical levels. From an epistemological point of view it refers to that which is called the complexity paradigm (Dupuy 1982, Bocchi and Ceruti 1985). In particular, the adoption without reciprocal exclusion of a global-external and of a local-internal point of view means representing both the networks and their individual, local nodes as systems open to any type of exchange, but operatively closed, i.e. essentially self-referential as far as the rules of their internal workings are concerned, therefore self-governing, aimed essentially at reproducing their own identity (Maturana and Varela 1985 and 1987, Demouchel and Dupuy 1983).

As a consequence, the local nodes will not be simple "parts" of the network (sub-systems whose properties are reducible to those of the global system) and the global network will not be the simple sum of the local parts of which it is composed. Not only will the local be unable to exist without the global, but the latter will also depend upon the very functioning of the various local systems.

More arduous is the practical problem, of the scheme implicit in substituting hypermodern geo-graphies with complex ones. The fortune of hypermodern geo-graphies is most certainly linked to the performative force of their representation.

The emphasis placed upon global levelling connections, upon the speed and fatality of change, the fragmentation of places and actors, upon the absence of local constraints and regulations, sounds like the legitimization of the social and political order that is dominant today on a planetary scale and at the same time, like a programme for an ever more capillary colonization of the planet, aimed at eliminating local resistances to standardization. It can be observed that, in such a way, a dialectic process is reduced to only one of its components and it is also probable that this networked globalization scheme has as little probability of ever being realized as did the too modern and too areal plan of Lenin when he dreamt of transforming an entire society into "one great office and into one giant factory".[6] However, there would appear to be no existing project today capable of re-balancing the dissymetry of social and cultural relationships between global and local levels.

Let us take as an example the classic problem of territorial justice. A *modern* type of geography of underdevelopment would see this in terms of "delay", or as a structural condition of capitalist development that cannot be eliminated unless it is acted upon globally. In both cases it means extending a global model at a local level according to the well known formula: "If a man is hungry, don't feed him fish but teach him how to catch some".

In *hypermodern* geo-graphies, such a problem is no longer posed: the loss of meaning of physical distance, the fragmentation of the old centre-periphery model, the mobility of information and flexible location all suggest the idea of diffuse opportunity, of local valorization wherever possible, even if not foreseeable or plannable. It is the access to the networks that counts, not geographic position or specific local features.

For a geography that recognizes the *complexity* of the relationship between global networks and local nodes, the local underdevelopment is, above all, a defect of what Maturana and Varela (1985) call the "structural coupling" of two systems. From an internal point of view, from within local systems, this defect will then make it im-

---

6 *State and Revolution, (Italian edition: Feltrinelli, Milano, 1970, p. 142).*

possible to transform local values into values exchangeable within global networks; this, not because local values do not exist (as would appear when observing the system from the outside), but because the relationships of existing networks prevent local values from becoming values of global exchange. The solution in this case is: "If a man is hungry, don't teach him how to fish, but exchange your fish for something he can produce". Or rather: do not try to reduce him to a part of your system, but allow him to *take part* in it in an autonomous manner. This means considering what is specific to the other as something we lack. Territorial equity is not merely equality, neither is it the elimination of differences, instead it is the valorization of diversity.

All this involves the possibility of reciprocal translation of local languages, their practical comprehension, the sharing of values produced in different contexts through unrepeatable experiences.

As is well-known, this is a complex theoretical problem that is still under debate also in the field of geographic studies. This has its counterpart in a no less serious, practical problem. Why, today, is it not only difficult to appreciate and therefore to desire what is different but even to tolerate it? To consider this as a resolvable problem on a purely pedagogical level would be to underestimate the dissymmetry in the balance of power in relationships which prevents most local systems from taking an active part in the construction of communication and exchange networks. On a global scale, representational space would appear to be saturated by a single language and a dominant values system (the previously mentioned inflated "local" European one), which not only represents itself but claims to represent all local ones as its own parts in a necessity/contingency relationship.

It is this performative representation which prevents local diversity from being recognized as such and that reduces local systems' request to the simple right to self-representation in their own dialect. But this precludes the possibility of translocal communication and therefore the chance of participating in a global network of exchanges while conserving one's own local identity and having it recognized.

None of the solutions proposed so far in the field of geographic-territorial studies would appear totally convincing. The suggestive proposals put forward by A. Magnaghi and the research group coordinated by him (Magnaghi 1990b) in terms of "city of villages", "ecopolis" and "higher local level" (Giusti 1990) would seem to underestimate the strength of hierarchical relationships between different territorial levels. Other solutions (Habermas' "communicative action" "structural coupling" of operatively closed systems, etc.) appear too optimistic on the subject of opportunities for communication and hence for the conciliation of conflicts between these levels (Mondada and Söderström 1990). More realistic, even if somewhat partial, is perhaps the proposal put forward by A. Pred (1989a, 1989b, 1990) of a resistance strategy of the "local" based upon the conflicts of meanings.

The problem remains open and presents itself as one of the fields in which the construction-deconstruction methods of geo-graphies may well prove fruitful.

References

Bocchi G, Ceruti M (Eds), 1985 *La sfida della complessità* (Feltrinelli, Milano)

Bunge W, 1966 *Theoretical Geography* (Gleerup, Lund)

Castells M, 1989 *The informational City. Information Technology, Economic Restructuring and Urban-Regional Process* (Basil Blackwell, Oxford)

Dematteis G, 1985a *Le metafore della Terra. La geografia umana tra mito e scienza* (Milano, Feltrinelli)

Dematteis G, 1985b, "Dans la tête de Janus. Reflexions sur le côté poétique de la géographie" in *Géotopiques. Actes du Colloque sur l'imagination géographique* Eds C Raffestin, JB Racine (Universités Lausanne-Genève) pp. 109-128

Dematteis G, 1987, "La géographie comme médiation linguistique", in *Actes du Colloque international: Les langages des représentation géographiques* Ed G Zanetto (Università, Venezia)

Dematteis G, 1991, "Global Networks, Local Cities", paper presented at the Conference on Communications and the Future of European Cities. Glasgow, U.K.

Derrida J, 1991 *L'autre cap* suivi de *La démocratie ajournée* (Les Edition de Minuit, Paris)

Dupuy JP, 1982 *Ordres et desordres. Euquête sur un nouveau paradigme* (Seuil, Paris)

Demouchel P, Dupuy JP (Eds), 1983 *Colloque de Cerisy. L'auto-organisation. De la physique au politique* (Seuil, Paris)

Farinelli F, 1989 *Pour une théorie générale de la géographie* (Université de Genève, Genève)

Farinelli F, 1981 "Storia del concetto geografico di paesaggio", in *Paesaggio. Immagine e realtà* (Electa, Milano) pp 151-158

Focault M, 1975 *Surveiller et punir. Naissance de la prison* (Gallimard, Paris)

Gadamer H, 1991 (german original, 1989) *L'eredità dell'Europa* (Einaudi, Torino)

Giusti M, 1990, "Locale, territorio, comunità , sviluppo. Appunti per un glossario", in *Il territorio dell'abitare* Ed A Magnaghi (Angeli, Milano)

Goddard JB, 1990 "The geography of the information economy", PICT Policy Research Papers 11, CURDS, University of Newcastle Upon Tyne

Gregory D, 1989, "Areal differentiation and post-modern human geography" in *Horizons in human geography*, Eds D Gregory, R Walford (Macmillan, London) pp 67-96

Harvey D, 1969 *Explanation in Geography* (Arnold, London).

Harvey D, 1989 *The Condition of Postmodermity. An Enquiry into the Origins of Cultural Change* (Basil Blackwell, Oxford)

King AD, 1990 *Global Cities. Post-imperialism and the Internationalization of London* (Routledge, London and New York)

Magnaghi A (Ed), 1990a *Il territorio dell'abitare. Lo sviluppo locale come alternativa strategica* (Angeli, Milano)

Magnaghi A, 1990b,"Dalla cosmopoli alla città di villaggi" in *La città e il limite. I confini della città* Ed G Paba (Usher, Firenze) pp 28-39

Maturana H, Varela F, 1985 (english original, 1980) *Autopoiesi e cognizione. La realizzazione del vivente* (Padova, Marsilio)

Maturana H, Varela F, 1987 *L'albero della conoscenza* (Garzanti, Milano)

Mondada L, Söderström O, 1990, "Communication et espace. Perspectives théoriques et enjeux sociaux", Cahiers du Département des Langues et des Sciences du Langage. Université de Lausanne, n. 11

Olsson G, 1980 *Birds in Eggs/Eggs in Bird* (Pion, London)

Olsson G, 1991a *Lines of power/Limits of language* (University of Minnesota Press, Minneapolis, Oxford)

Olsson G, 1991b *Linee senza ombra. La tragedia della pianificazione* (Theoria, Roma)

Olsson G, 1991c "Invisible Maps. A Prospectus", *Geografiska Annaler 73*.B, 85-91

Pred A, 1989a, "Survey 14: the Locally Spoken Word and Local Struggles". *Environment and Planning D: Society and Space, 7,* 211-233

Pred A, 1989b *Lost Words and Lost Worlds: Modernity and the Language of Everyday Life in Late Nineteenth Century Stockholm,* (Cambridge University Press, Cambridge)

Pred A, 1990 *Making Histories and Constructing Human Geographies* (Westway Press, Boulder Col.)

Raffestin C, 1981 *Per una geografia del potere* (Unicopli, Milano)

Raffestin C, 1984, "Territorializzazione, deterritorializzazione, riterritorializzazione e informazione", in *Regione e regionalizzazione* Ed A Turco (Angeli, Milano) pp 69.82

Schmitt K, 1974 *Der Nomos der Erde im Völkerrecht des Jus Publicum Europaeum* (Duncker Humblot, Berlin)

Serres M, 1980 *Hermes V. Le passage du Nord-Ouest* (Les Editions de Minuit, Paris)

Soja EW, 1989 *Postmodern Geographies. The Reassertion of Space in Critical Social Theory* (Verso, London)

Toulmin S, 1990 *Cosmopolis: the Hidden Agenda of Modernity* (The Free Press, New York)

Vidal De La Blache P, 1903 *Tableau géographique de la France* (Reprint: Libr. J Tallandier, Paris 1979, p. 8).

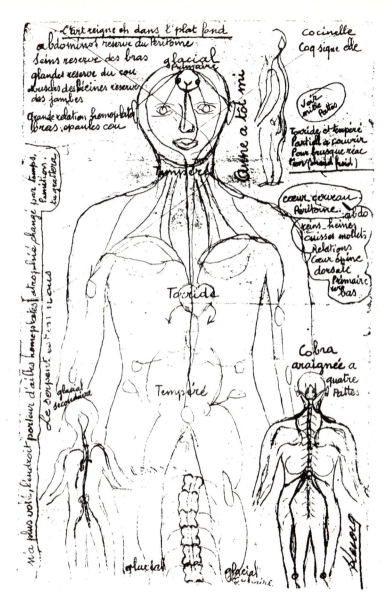

Sylvain: *"L'art reigne eh dans l'plat fond"*

EPILOGUE

That evening the three had come together to eat the castrato and to talk. It was in Castel San Pietro and the Thai wife of the innkeeper was just bringing a bottle of wine. Two years had passed since they had last met in Italy, and now their book was almost finished. Leaning back in their chairs, they felt the pleasant tiredness after a full day. "So, how would you conclude?" one of them said. "I don't want to conclude! There is still so much going on," the other replied. "But – do you know," she asked the third, "what exactly does *epilogue* mean?" "It comes from the Greek *epilogos*, from *epilegein*, that is *to add, to say something further*." "So it is not about concluding, but about continuing... I am glad I don't have to pretend I could say what the book is about! But what should I add?" "Well, said the other,"while you were putting all the texts together, what were the questions that came to your mind?" "Many questions!" "Dica," the third one provoked her, "what were your questions?"

"In the conceptions of human existence proposed there, existence in thought-and-action, in the landscape of language, or in the utopia and the boundary, there certainly are many things that I cannot grasp. And yet, having read the texts several times, I always read new things into them. It is as if they did not contain answers, but continuously brought about a reformulation of my questions. Now, for example, I ask myself what types of silence are there? Can one speak a language of silence? Is there not precise communication even beyond the limits of representational language?

And then: If it is true that the tradition of representational thinking is the tradition of Geography ..." "Some more?" One of the others was refilling the glasses. "No, I have had enough. Well, if the tradition is such – and I believe that it is – what can Geography tell us about the critical presumptions of representational thinking? Yes, the old maps do not work any more, existing forms of political representation are in trouble, there is a social and individual identity crisis, now the master-discourse feels the need to justify itself... many different sides of the crisis of representation are discussed in this book. But does this crisis mark the transition from one

217

particular form of representation to another, from a territorial form to one of topological power-networks, for example, or do the limits of representation lie deeper? Do they lie even in the surface itself, in the table which carries the spatial arrangement?" "But the table is of course the map", the other said. "And it is the graven image, the taboo" added the third. "Yes," he replied, "and it is the table of the sacrifice on which the living body turns into a corpse." "Ecco, your castrato!" the innkeeper's wife came just in time. They had been very hungry already. "Can you pass me your plate?" "The plate?" asked the third, still involved in her questions. "Could we not communicate without having such a plain, such an altar, such a map? If the limits of language exceed the limits of representation, do they then have to coincide with that plain? But even if it were the case, perhaps the plain of dimensions will be replaced by the surface of the sea, by a medium that changes with changes in the different realms it connects? – Well, let us eat! – It is just that to me, the problem is not the crisis of representation, but representation as such: conceiving of thinking and speaking just in terms of representation, this is the problem!" "Oh, that looks very good! Let's eat!" "Yes, buon appetito!"

When they had finished eating, one of them asked: "So, how would you conclude this epilogue?" "I don't know. The outlooks of the people who have written in the book are quite different. I don't want to bundle them all into one thread." "Of course we have different perspectives! And of course it should not be otherwise." "But then," suggested the third, "you should try to tell a story, because a story is a tissue of different threads woven into each other." "Come on," she said, "it is you, who are the story-teller!" "No, no, it should be a woman! This is even stated in our book." – "Well, I have heard a good story, and I also think that it could be appropriate... but it has been told so wonderfully, impossible to repeat it!" "Don't worry! Stories cannot be repeated, they are always told for the first time. It is your story in any case. Let me just order another bottle of wine before you begin!"

"All right. It is a story about Jesus, but it is not about religion, it rather is... well, you will hear it: Once upon a time Jesus wanted to come back to the earth for a while to visit his people. It was – do you remember? – in 1556, and he had choosen Sevilla, which then was the capital of the Inquisition. So he came down to the white-hot squares of the southern city. Silently and unobtrusively he walked, but... but everyone immediately recognized Him! They gathered around Him and followed Him, brought their ill relatives, and, as he used to do, He blessed and healed them. That was happening on the square in front of the Cathedral as, just then, the Cardinal Grand Inquisitor walked by. He was an old man, upright and with a withered face, dressed in a monk's cowl. Immediately he saw what was going on. Pointing with his finger to Jesus, he ordered his guards to arrest and imprison Him.

Then, in the middle of the night, the Great Inquisitor went down to the dungeon to see his prisoner. 'Why did you come and disturb us,' he asked, 'you do not have the right to add anything to that which you have said before! Standing in front of Him he closed his eyes: 'You probably know that tomorrow morning I will judge you and you will be burned on the funeral pile.' Jesus looked at him and was silent. Then the old man continued. 'How would you tell the human beings anything without profoundly contradicting yourself,' he asked. 'It would take away their freedom, this human freedom which used to be so important to you.' Then he..."

"Oh," one of the others interrupted her, "don't you know a story that is a little less heavy? After a meal like that...!" "Well, after a book like that...!" "Alright." So she went on.

"Then the Grand Inquisitor looked sternly at Jesus: 'This freedom has cost the human beings fifteen hundred years of struggle and suffering,' he said. 'Have you not known that? Why did not you listen to this powerful spirit?' – He meant the spirit of Negativity from the Bible. – 'Three times he spoke to you, and three times you refused! There in the desert he had recommended you to give people bread instead of ideas, and to be their Lord and tell them what to live for instead of demanding that they should decide it with their hearts. Later he carried you up on the roof of the temple and asked you to do a miracle. He knew that human beings need to believe in the power of the miracle to calm their consciousness. Then he even showed you all the empires of the world and called you to be king of all of them. Did you not know that men would not stop fighting each other before they would not all have one common ruler? How could you not know the contradictions of human existence! You, who love human beings so much, how could you give them a duty as heavy as this?'

The old man had kept talking at Jesus. Now that he had finished, he waited for the prisoner to reply. But He just sat there and looked quietly at him. 'So hear then,' the Grand Inquisitor said, 'we have taken it upon us. We have told them what is right and what is wrong, we have given them the miracle, and we will not hesitate when it comes to being the authority that unites the world. - And the people have come. They have brought us their freedom. Humbly they left it at our feet so that we would make them happy. To us they confess their problems and we decide about them in the name of truth. In His name. For we are not with you, we are with Him. This is our secret!' The old man paused for a while. With a lower voice he continued: 'You know that. And you also know that we are not doing it because we enjoy this power. We cannot enjoy it because we know its secret. But we keep it because we love human beings. - Because we love them all, not just some of them! Maybe there is one who is strong enough for your freedom, maybe there are a thousand, but the others? If you had respected humans less, you would have come closer to loving them!' There the old man stopped. He had noticed that for the whole time the prisoner had been listening carefully. Now He calmly looked into his eyes. The old man hoped that now He would say something."

"And?" "No end. This is where the story will continue. But later, and not told by me." "Well," one of the listeners asked the other, "what do you think?" "I think we have to finish the wine." And so they stayed on for a bit, sitting in this restaurant on the square, right under the eyes of Saint Pietro, who was quietly standing there on his column, lit by a circular halo of neon-light.

Dagmar Reichert

LIST OF CONTRIBUTORS

Giuseppe Dematteis
Dipartimento Interateneo Territorio, Politecnico è Università di Torino, Viale Mattioli 39, I-10125, Torino, ITALIA

Franco Farinelli
Istituto di Geografia,Università di Bologna, Via San Giacomo 3, I-40126 Bologna ITALIA

Peter Gould
Department of Geography, Penn State University, University Park, PA 16802 USA

Matthew Hannah
Department of Geography, Penn State University, University Park, PA 16802 USA

Ole Michael Jensen
Statens Byggeforskningsinstitut, SBI Postboks 119, Hoersholm, DK-2970, DENMARK

Verena Meier
Geographisches Institut, Klingelbergstr. 16, CH-4056 Basel, SWITZERLAND

Mario Neve
Istituto di Geografia,Università di Bologna, S.S.L.M.I.T., Corso della Repubblica, 136, I-47100 Forli, ITALIA

Gunnar Olsson
Nordplan, Box 1658, Stockholm, S-11186, SWEDEN

Allan Pred
Department of Geography, University of California, Berkeley, California, CA-94720 USA

Dagmar Reichert
Geographisches Institut, ETH Zürich, Winterthurerstr. 190, CH-8057 Zürich, SCHWEIZ

Ola Söderström
Institut de Geographie, Universite de Lausanne,
B.F.S.H.2 - Dorigny, CH-1015 Lausanne, SCHWEIZ
Ulf Strohmayer
Department of Geography, Penn State University, University Park, PA 16802 USA

Rafael Ramirez,
The Beauty of Social Organization

Studies of Action and Organization (SAO), Vol. 4

ISBN 3-89265-009-8, 167 pages
DM36.00, ÖS 288.00, SFR 36,00, US$ 24,60

This book is about beauty.

There are no recipes for beauty. However, there are experiences which help to understand what we mean by **beauty.**

Understanding beauty as a rational process, as is here proposed, provides an understanding of organizations which has not been available so far. This book contains the very first aesthetic theory of social organization.

The book is of interest to organizational analysts, organizational sociologists, social psychologists, philosophers and consultants, economists, managers, and everybody concerned with appreciating and understanding organizations in **innovative ways.**

Published by
ACCEDO, Gnesener Str. 1, D-81929 Munich.

Pierre Guillet de Monthoux
ACTION AND EXISTENCE: Anarchism for Business Admistration
(Second Edition)
Studies of Action and Organization (SAO), Vol. 3
*ISBN 3-89265-008-X 269 pages,
DM 44.00, ÖS 352.00, SFR 44.00, US $ 31,50*

"Amusing, stimulating, a vivid description of living issues! Pierre Guillet de Monthoux demonstrates that writing about management theory is not always as dry as dust nor full of jargon." *(MDU Bulletin, September 1983)*

"The author does not pretend to be flat and 'objektive'; he has values, opinions and wants to present them. For readers of classical taxtbooks there is a danger here. This book won't be a good companian to fall asleep with after a long working day! It is lively rich, and I would also say in these days where..." *(Jean de Kervasdoué, Organisational Studies, August 1985)*

"The approach is heavily jocular as might be expected froma professor at a Swedish business school. But for people interested (and who isn't) in problems of the hierarchical bureaucracy that surround us, it is a refreshingly different approach."*(Colin Ward, New Society, September 1983)*

Published by
ACCEDO, Gnesener Str. 1, D-81929 Munich 81.